Victory has become a proven res
set forth in her first book, *Shatt*
greater dimension to those truth
Strongholds. We are challenged
setting us free, showing us how to continue using these tools in becoming men
and women of the Kingdom. I highly recommend this book to all believers
today who want to be on the cutting edge of the moving of God.

– Iverna Tompkins,
Internationally known speaker and author

Liberty has done it again! *BEYOND Shattered Strongholds* will indeed help
people rise to a higher level of living for Jesus! We highly recommend this
book to our Christian counselors to use for their own personal growth.
We also believe that it is an excellent book for their counselees to read. We
believe in Liberty's message so much that we have personally purchased
hundreds of her books and gave them to our counselors as additional tools
to aid in their counseling efforts.

– Drs. Richard and Phyllis Arno
National Christian Counselors Association, Sarasota, Florida

Few things have impacted our church with such transformational power
and influence as Liberty Savard's teaching on binding and loosing. It has
created a culture of freedom for those who have lived under the oppression
of habitual sin, generational bondages, and emotional pain. However,
the true beauty of her writing lies within Liberty's sincere desire for the
success of her fellow man. If you're looking for life change and spiritual
empowerment, you'll find it within the genius of her pages of this book,
BEYOND Shattered Strongholds.

– Senior Co-Pastor Kyle Horner
River of Life Worship Center, Cherry Hill, New Jersey

Wow, this new book is the perfect follow up to *Shattering Your Strongholds*.
My first exposure to Reverend Savard's books came at a time of intense crisis
in my life. The principles of the message she teaches and her patience as a
mentor to me rescued my life and my ministry from self-destruction when
I began applying this message to my life. The awesome thing about this
new book *BEYOND Shattered Strongholds* is its inspirational message
to get on with that which God has called us all to do. Okay, so you've
shattered your strongholds. Well, now get on with producing the fruit that
God has called you to bear right in your own backyard! Thanks, Liberty,
for continuing to instruct us in how to become the vessels we need to be
to minister to our generation.

– Senior Pastor R. Tony McGhee
Wilmington Christian Center, Wilmington, North Carolina

The truths I have uncovered through reading Liberty Savard's *Shattering Your Strongholds* series have been life-changing! They have been an enormous help to me in my own walk, and have helped equip me as a pastor and teacher more than ANY other resource. In *BEYOND Shattered Strongholds*, Reverend Savard gives practical tools and timely insights which will stretch every reader to go beyond himself and become the tangible expression of Jesus Christ. I have yet to meet someone who has read these books whose life has not been catapulted to a new level of living!

– Senior Co-Pastor Danielle Horner
River of Life Worship Center, Cherry Hill, New Jersey

Liberty has once again taken a deep mystery and made it understandable and useable in her newest book *BEYOND Shattered Strongholds*. This book will take you to a higher realm of victory over your soul with greater fruitfulness in Kingdom life. Liberty has a way of teaching foundational truths, infused with fresh revelation, that make you feel compelled to take immediate action. Then she breaks down those truths and lays out an understanding of how you can walk them out in your own life.

Liberty uses mini-parables to compare unique insights from life to a practical understanding of your own life. Principles of love, patience, and even influencing the family are all in here, as well as my favorite chapter "Get Ready to Influence the World!" Her writing style is humorous, progressive, hard-hitting, and passionate. This book is so anointed! She ranks at the top in my book when it comes to teaching in a way that transforms you from the inside out, while keeping you fully engaged.

Liberty lives and breathes an invigorating zeal for the body of Christ, I can say this from a first-hand basis! I've known Liberty for almost ten years and she is a mesmerizing fireball for God in our generation. I highly recommend both author and this timely book to everyone who wants to seize their destiny.

– Sean Smith, President of Sean Smith Ministries,
Author of Prophetic Evangelism

In *BEYOND Shattered Strongholds*, Liberty Savard gives deeper purpose to the binding and loosing keys, enabling you to move from freedom to God-ordained fruitfulness. Grasp and walk in the principles outlined in this book and you will become a powerhouse of productivity for the Kingdom of God as you step out of your own issues and begin to understand your dynamic, ongoing purpose to influence the age in which you live.

– Brenda Parshotam, Founder and Director
Life Impact, New Zealand

BEYOND
Shattered
Strongholds

BEYOND
Shattered
Strongholds

Liberty S. Savard

Bridge-Logos
Orlando, Florida 32822

Bridge-Logos
Orlando, FL 32822 USA

BEYOND Shattered Strongholds
by Liberty Savard

Printed in the United States of America.

Library of Congress Catalog Card Number: 2007939242
International Standard Book Number 978-0-88270-023-6

Scriptures in the book are from Biblesoft's PC Study Bible Version 4.1

TM is for The Message
AMP is for The Amplified Version
NIV is for the New International Version
NKJV is for the New King James Version
KJV is for the original King James Version
NAS is for the New American Standard Bible

G616.318.B.m710.35230

Dedication

This book is dedicated to all of God's fruit bearers
in this generation.

Contents

Preface

This book was first conceived as an updated version of my first book, *Shattering Your Strongholds*, published in 1992. I could not decide whether to write a pure update or a stand-alone book with the best of the original along with the progression of the message over the last twenty years. It was hard to think of omitting so many things in the original *Shattering Your Strongholds*. I am a firm believer in the old axiom: If it ain't broke, don't try to fix it.

However, the progression of this message over the past two decades, along with working with so many using the binding and loosing prayers, made me realize that there was a greater goal of this message. That goal was not to just make your Christian walk more fulfilling, and not to just to teach you how to pray more effectively.

The ultimate goal of this message is cause you to go on into your destiny of influencing your generation for the Kingdom on a larger scale than you ever dreamed possible.

This book has been written to tell you what lies beyond learning how to pray the binding and loosing prayers—what lies beyond the surrender of your soul. It is a call to step up to what you have always been called to do in this age. Your destiny is far beyond feeling secure and peaceful, far beyond good church attendance, and far beyond being kind to your neighbors. You are good seed filled with divine energy that has the potential to produce bushels of fruit.

You have been sown into this age to bear fruit for the Kingdom of God. You have been planted where you are to be a world changer and an influence for Him. This book is a call to come way up beyond worrying about your job, worrying about your finances, and fretting over your relationships.

This is a call to stop being like the man who looked in the mirror, realized part of who he was, but then walked away forgetting what he had seen. We have all gone to church or to meetings where we were stirred and uplifted by the preacher's exhortations. We briefly saw ourselves reflected in the preacher's call to come up to a higher place, but then we walked away forgetting what we had seen and heard.

This is a call to go beyond applying this message just to your own life. It is a call to move out into the world to influence this generation. If you only read these pages to see yourself reflected in them and then put it down and walk away unchanged, I have failed. I have specifically failed to cause the pilot light of your faith to ignite your destiny purposes for being in the world at this time.

Please set yourself to look BEYOND who you think you are and where you have been up until now. Get a vision of who Jesus says you are—good seed destined to grow and bear much fruit for the Kingdom of God.

Acknowledgments

I would like to acknowledge Rev. Karen Failor's encouragement, feedback, and proofreading of my work on this manuscript with many e-mails and instant messages going back and forth from Sacramento, California to Fort Wayne, Indiana— sometimes long into the wee hours of the morning. I would also like to acknowledge Pastors Kyle and Danielle Horner of River of Life Worship Center in Cherry Hill, New Jersey. They freely shared their style of ministry with me through interviews and e-mails, allowing me to incorporate all they shared into the final chapter of this book. Kyle and Danielle, you are first class fruit bearers!

"I chose you,
and put you in the world to bear fruit,
fruit that won't spoil."

John 15:16, The Message

Chapter 1

Just What Is BEYOND Your Shattered Strongholds?

Launch Pad to the World!

How exciting it is to write an update on this message about Matthew 16:19 and the Keys of the Kingdom prayer principles. From the first sharing of this message in 1986, people have declared a new freedom in their Christian walk with some even saying it was the first time they felt really free since they became born again. Let me share a few recent testimonies here:

> When I read SYS, it opened a whole new understanding of why I was the way I was in many areas. God has healed me in places where I didn't even know I was wounded. My husband and I have now reconciled and have a ministry of recovery and restoration of relationships using the SYS trilogy in our teachings. – Dana

> Thank you so much for these books. I reread them regularly and use these principles to keep my own life on track. J.K.

> I believe the Spirit of God has touched my life deeply through reading your books. I am now more aware of the strongholds that have been keeping me from understanding the deep truths of God's Word. Thank you for the answer. – Joanne, United Kingdom

I am an Episcopal priest on the East Coast seeking a way
to lead my people deeper in Him. I asked a priest in the
south who would be God's instrument for such a deeper
walk. He said that your message was so significant for their
church that I should contact you. – Matthew

I have read all of your books and I think that you are on the
money. I have gleaned more from your books than many
years of professional training! Keep up the fight!
– D. I., Licensed Counselor

This morning I saw you on TBN and was taken by a
woman speaking in a very down-to-earth manner about real
things. I have been convicted by God to make a positive
difference with the rest of my life. I am a 46-year-old man,
divorced with three children. Listening to your message
of the Keys of the Kingdom prayers has encouraged me.
– Christopher

I am in leadership in a large Methodist church and it was
great timing for the Keys of the Kingdom leadership prayer
you sent me. After all, what is the point of running on
human power when God power is so available! Thanks for
hitting the heart of it. – Shelby

I have been a Christian for 48 years. I have always felt there
was something missing in my prayer life and your books
have been a revelation to me! I will keep logging onto your
website for guidance and encouragement. – C. Australia

I can't describe the thrill this new adventure has been for me
as I have prayed with the binding and loosing keys. I have
been walking with Jesus for nearly 20 years and these last
4 months of praying this way has changed my life! I pray
that the Church will embrace this truth. – T.N.

Matthew 16:19 tells us that Jesus said He was giving us
the Keys to the Kingdom of heaven—whatever we would

bind on earth would be bound in heaven and whatever we would loose on earth would be loosed in heaven. This is a powerful promise with endless positive possibilities! You can bind your will to the will of the Father to obligate yourself to His purposes. You can bind your mind to the mind of Christ to align your thoughts with His. You can bind your emotions to the healing balance of the Holy Spirit so that they can be healed.

You can loose wrong thoughts, wrong beliefs, wrong patterns of thinking, word curses, and the effects and influences of wrong agreements from your soul. You can loose the works of the enemy from yourself and from others.

The only "catch" to praying this way is that you need to bind and loose that which has already been bound and loosed in heaven according to God's pre-

> You can actually cause things on earth to come into alignment with God's will that is already established in heaven. How exciting is that?

established will. We don't know near as much as we think we do about God's will for every situation, so the "training wheel" binding and loosing prayers in this book are always specific to what God wants. They are never specific to what your soul and mine might want.

Training wheels are balance and forward motion aids (just like learning to ride a bicycle) that help you learn how to do something new. When you no longer need them, pray with these principles on your own.

God has always wanted us to pray in agreement with Him that His wisdom, goodness, power, and love are always directed towards us and those we pray for. If you have not known how to pray effectively in agreement with God's will and purposes, you can start doing so before you finish this chapter.

What Lies BEYOND Shattered Strongholds?

Some who have prayed with these Keys of the Kingdom prayer principles get so excited about being able to finally surrender the baggage of their souls that they want to build a memorial to the fact that they have begun to rid themselves of their old ways of behaving and reacting. This surely is a place of victory, but it is not the place to stop, drop, and roll out a memorial! Beyond your shattered strongholds is where you begin to produce the most important thing you will ever produce in your Christian walk:

FRUIT FOR THE KINGDOM OF GOD!

In 2005, I returned from a meeting of pastors, traveling ministries, and Bible teachers with a new vision of what God wanted from me and from you. I understood more about what was BEYOND binding myself to the will of God and the mind of Christ—BEYOND the shattering of strongholds, the loosing of preconceived ideas, and the loosing of religious and generational bondage thinking. BEYOND all of these accomplishments was a surrendered soul, which would seek to align itself with God's plans and purposes.

A parable is the comparison of an abstract concept to actual things that people understand. The parable of the seed and the sower found in both Luke's Gospel and Matthew's Gospel sound alike at first reading, but they are different. God's Word often works on many different levels, building precept upon precept, line upon line.

Luke's recording of this parable tells us of the Word of God (Luke 8:11-15) being cast into the hearts of men and women. Whether or not the Word of God will grow and bear fruit appears to depend upon the condition of the soil. These passages do not speak of the effectiveness of the Word that has been sown, but rather the condition of the hearts into which it was sown.

This had always been somewhat disheartening to me because it meant that you could sow the Word of God faithfully and perhaps only 25 percent (four types of soil) of your sowing had a chance to take root. But we read in Matthew's Gospel that Jesus said this to His disciples about the parable of the seed and the sower (Matthew 13:37-38, NIV):

> *"The one who sowed the good seed is the Son of Man. The field is the world, and the good seed stands for the sons of the kingdom."*

Jesus is saying here that He was going to sow the sons and daughters of the Kingdom into the world to bear fruit. We are the ones Jesus desires to cast into the world to bear fruit wherever He chooses to plant us. God sowed His Son into this world to influence humanity and to produce fruit for the Kingdom. Now we have been sown into this world to influence humanity in the age in which we live and to produce fruit for the Kingdom.

God desires that we would influence those in the world at this time, finishing the works that Jesus left for us to do after He went to be with His Father. This is very exciting to me—I'm a good seed of influence divinely planted right where I am—a good seed that can produce good fruit! I've been sown into the world where God wants me to be, and I'm going to do my best to bloom like crazy where He's planted me. So can you!

We go to church to learn, to be discipled, to have godly fellowship, and to be trained for greater purposes. Unfortunately, some of us have been taught to avoid mingling with those in the world—yet the world is our mission field! Notice in Matthew 13:28-29 where the owner's servants asked the owner if they should pull up the tares (weeds) that an enemy had sown into his field overnight. The owner said to leave them alone and let the harvesters deal with them at the time of the harvest.

> Our main sphere of influence should be out in the world.

The field of this owner represents the world, and the tares represent unbelievers. We are not to judge the tares and put them away from us. The harvesters (angels) at the end of the age will deal with those who are still unbelievers when Christ returns. Until He does, we are to influence potential wheat and tares alike—always hoping that some of the tares might come over to God's side.

Struggling Seeds and Fruitless Lives

This commission is a really big deal! I have heard so many times that we are to bear fruit, but I am finally getting it— finally seeing that we are all called to be world influencers and world changers. Now that's some kind of fruit!

It can be very difficult for believers who are still filled with strongholds, biases, fears, unforgiveness, unmet needs, unhealed hurts, and unresolved issues to understand that they have been sown into this world to influence it for the Kingdom of God. Hurting, wounded believers are often self-focused with little vision for anything beyond their own protection. Such believers are like seeds that have bacteria and mold inside of them, working against their destiny purpose of producing fruit. The good seed (Matthew 13:37-38) is the seed that has no such hindrances to being fruitful.

Now, here's good news! You can strip these infected, moldy, old thought patterns, fears, and biases right out of your soul—in fact, you must. Rarely will God forcibly take our wrong thoughts, bad attitudes, and prejudices from us, if ever. He keeps calling them to our attention while asking us to put them away as in Ephesians 4:22-26 (NKJV):

> *"Put off, concerning your former conduct, the old man which grows corrupt according to the deceitful lusts, and be renewed in the spirit of your mind . . . . Put away lying, let each one of you speak truth with his neighbor, for we are members of one another. Be angry, and do not sin: do not let the sun go down on your wrath."*

Fruit Bearers Need Pruning

We have all heard messages and stories from the Bible about bearing fruit. Nice stories, comforting stories actually, until they venture into the area of the Father pruning the branches on the vine. In John 15:1-2 (TM), Jesus said:

> *"I am the Real Vine and my Father is the Farmer. He cuts off every branch of me that doesn't bear grapes. And every branch that is grape-bearing he prunes back so it will bear even more."*

Agricultural pruning (which Jesus used as a concrete example to explain the pruning that God would do to us) removes or reduces certain plant parts that are not required, that are no longer effective, or that are of no use to the plant. It is done to supply additional nutrition and energy to the remaining part of the plant for more fruitfulness.

Ouch! Pruning can be painful, but it is productive. Pruning increases the vine's (and our) ability to produce an even greater harvest of fruit. Thank heavens the Lord doesn't prune us with big old metal pruning shears like human vineyard owners use.

How does God prune us? He first speaks to us about pruning ourselves, about putting off the useless, sickly, and diseased parts of our souls. When we don't listen to Him, He allows us to go through difficult circumstances over and over until we are forced to see the useless, ineffective things that are sucking the strength and life out of us. If we begin to loose and cut (the easy way) these things from ourselves voluntarily, God won't have to run us through the learning process over and over until we eventually "get it" (the hard way).

> God doesn't want to have to keep protecting us from people who make us feel unloved and misunderstood— He wants to heal us so we don't react to any hard thing someone

For example, if we are packing a lot of anger, God often allows repeated situations with people who always make us angry. If we are packing garbage bags full of unforgiveness, God may allow streams of people to come around us who blame us for everything. He will try to show us that we have some areas weakening us that we need to let go of so He can strengthen and build us up. This is so we can influence others positively rather than being influenced by their negative issues.

He is also showing us that what we sow is what we will reap. If we nurture and fertilize and water our own anger or unforgiveness, guess what fruit will grow up in our unsurrendered souls? Guess what kind of fruit we will be exhibiting to others we come into contact with? Sowing of seeds always produces like kinds of fruit having seeds that produce like kinds of fruit that have seeds that produce like kinds of fruit, and on and on.

Another good reason for getting stronghold thinking, anger, unforgiveness, and bad attitudes out of your soul is so you won't have any landing strips for incoming darts and daggers—from people or from the enemy. Proverbs 26:2 tells us:

> *"Curses cannot hurt you unless you deserve them. They are like birds that fly by and never light" (TEV).*

This book is all about giving you keys to prayer that will help you to rip up those negative landing strips in your own soul!

Why doesn't God just tell you what to let go of instead of having to show you through uncomfortable situations and circumstances? He has—over and over again—in His Word. Unfortunately, we don't always see ourselves in His admonitions and warnings; we don't "get it" that He's talking to us about our need to let go of our wrong thinking and bad attitudes.

Keys of the Kingdom

Aren't you grateful that God's wonderful plan of salvation, His divine gift of forgiveness and freedom, was given to you? Nothing you ever did earned you this gift; it was a pure gifting. When we learn how to cooperate with the Giver, the entire process of our salvation is the act of embracing what He does for us and through us. Romans 10:9 (TM) says this:

> *"Say the welcoming word to God—'Jesus is my Master'—embracing, body and soul, God's work of doing in us what he did in raising Jesus from the dead. That's it. You're not 'doing' anything; you're simply calling out to God, trusting him to do it for you. That's salvation."*

Just as you have to unwrap and open up other packages to use or wear the gift inside of them, you also need to open this divine gift up and put it on. Jesus has provided a way for you to experience all of the goodness in this divine package. He's also provided a way for you to get rid of everything that tries to drag you down and hold you back from this gift's purposes! That provision is the Keys of the Kingdom in Matthew 16:19 (NKJV). Jesus said:

> *"I will give you the Keys of the Kingdom, whatever you bind on earth will be bound in heaven, and whatever you loose on earth will be loosed in heaven."*

Jesus has given us these supernatural keys to enable us to bring our lives into alignment with God's plans for us. These keys allow us to stabilize and steady our lives by binding ourselves to His will. They help us to hear the thoughts and intents of the mind and heart of Jesus when we bind our minds to His mind. These keys position us for the healing of our wounded and hurt feelings when we bind our emotions to the healing balance of the Holy Spirit, our Comforter.

If this book could have been wired for sound, there would have been an audio cut of a flushing toilet right here to wmake sure you get the picture of what you can do with the broken rubble and junk in your soul!

With these keys, we can cut loose all of our wrong beliefs, our unforgiveness, our doubts, our misconceptions, and preformed mind sets, putting them away from ourselves forever if we choose to. We can open up our pain to Him and then walk away from a divine transaction filled with His power, grace, and love. As we pray with these keys, our souls can be flushed free of all old bondage thinking, prejudices, and fears that the world or the devil could tap into to put us in bondage.

Christ's giving of these keys in the first part of Matthew 16:19 represents the giving of permission, authority, and ability to enter into the kingdom of heaven to transact spiritual business according to the will of God. The last part of this verse reveals *how* to transact that spiritual business. We pray with these keys to cause things on earth to come into alignment with God's established plans and purposes in heaven. Jesus prayed this in the Lord's Prayer in Luke 11:1-2 (KJV):

> *"And it came to pass, that, as he was praying in a certain place, when he ceased, one of his disciples said unto him, **Lord, teach us to pray**, as John also taught his disciples. And he said unto them, When ye pray, say, Our Father which art in heaven, Hallowed be thy name. Thy kingdom come. **Thy will be done, as in heaven, so in earth.**"*

The Power in the Keys

In the Scriptures the word "key" is used figuratively for power; it is also used as a sign of official authority. In Luke 11:52 (KJV), Jesus spoke to the Pharisees about the key of knowledge:

"Woe unto you, lawyers! for ye have taken away the key of knowledge: ye entered not in yourselves, and them that were entering in ye hindered."

The Pharisees jealously guarded the key of knowledge of spiritual things, distorting rather than revealing the truth of God's love and His life-saving guidance and direction for their lives. The religious leaders put great burdens upon the Jewish people when they prevented them from understanding the truth. It is sin to deliberately keep people from knowing truth.

Jesus Christ has given supernatural keys of power and authority to His believers to enable us to surrender to the good plans and great blessings of God. This act of surrender is not the sacrifice of becoming a puppet or a robot. It is the surrender of all wrong things in our souls that have persistently drained us of joy and hope: deceptions, wrong beliefs, wrong teachings, doubts, and distortions of truth that have infected our unsurrendered souls.

Jesus knew that we would have to live out our days on this rough and tumble earth after He was gone. So, He has made it possible for us to do this with His power and the Keys of the Kingdom.

Jesus experienced pain, want, hunger, fatigue, sorrow, and loss as He walked this earth in human form. He knew the sting of rejection, hatred, and sarcasm. He knows exactly what life feels like as a baby, a child, a teenager, and an adult. We are told in Galatians that in Christ Jesus there is no distinction between male and female (Galatians 3:28). He knows exactly how men, women, teenagers, and children think and feel in every hard situation of life.

Jesus knew that we would need the Keys of the Kingdom to break away from the baggage of our pasts and to destroy the works of the enemy

> Jesus did not suddenly come into this world as a full-grown Savior; He experienced all of the stages of life here on earth.

before we could fully face our future with purpose and hope. We all have a definite purpose in our futures. We are not just being scored on how well we do as we face all of life's tests down here. We are here to show God's love to the world, a divine love that has a hard time getting through His kids' minds when they are so filled with wrong thoughts and bad attitudes.

What's In Your Mind?

Most Christians would like to think that their minds are at least partly filled with the lofty things of God and high thoughts of praise and worship. The reality is that your mind is probably also quite cluttered with unanswered questions, unresolved feelings, unsettling memories, and somewhat skewed perceptions of everything you've ever seen, heard, and experienced.

This clutter can create a serious traffic jam that will hinder your ability to communicate with God.

Being born again did not instantly give you a renewed mind. Unless you experienced a sovereign overhaul on your soul by God (which He certainly *can* do if He chooses to), you probably still have much of the same clutter that you had in your mind before your new birth. Most people do. Acquiring a renewed mind comes only through the process of spending time in the Word, prayer and communion with God, and the application of good spiritual teachings.

The unrenewed mind (the mind still filled with soulish clutter) is always grounded in the natural, non-spiritual things of the world.

Your mind's renewal is enhanced and quickened when you consistently reject wrong patterns of thinking and wrong beliefs, focusing instead on things that are honest, just, pure, lovely, and of good report (Philippians 4:8, KJV).

You absolutely *can* reject and release wrong attitudes, wrong thought patterns, and wrong beliefs from your mind. This is not an abstract statement; it is a statement that has powerful prayer keys to back it up starting right now if you choose to try it. Everyone has some wrong attitude or thought in their mind that simply does not leave because they tell it to. It probably is being reinforced daily through rubbing up against other people with wrong attitudes and thoughts.

But what if you could free your mind from worldly attitudes and wrong beliefs even though you must still deal with and walk through some of society's most cranky, pushy situations every day? You could save yourself and those around you a lot of grief if you could, couldn't you?

You might disagree that your mind even contains any wrong thinking. Have you ever insisted, "God would never ask me to (you fill in the blank) _____"? What would you do if He did? Would you think, "God, why have you forsaken me? You know that I can't do this!"

Too many believers desperately want to believe that God would never ask them to confront their fears in order to do anything outside of their beliefs about themselves. Such wrong thoughts come from old patterns of thinking and misconceptions of God's truth. God *will* ask us to do things we think are beyond our capabilities.

If His purposes for us weren't beyond our abilities, why would we need Him? He wants us to let Him give us the strength, power, and courage to do anything He asks us to do. If your soul is filled with old fears and bad memories, it is not easy to trust God to give you His deeper truths in stages you can handle.

> As you continue to seek His truth, you begin to believe that He will empower you to do what He asks of you.

Every Christian knows the basic truth that Jesus died so that he or she could be forgiven and go to heaven. You and I can make it all the way home to Jesus by believing that. But what about the times when the struggles and temptations of life are clamoring so loudly in your face, you wonder how that truth will help you survive the here and now?

That is when you need to move beyond your surface understanding of what God wants you to know into the deeper realities of His truth received and believed. You may be very surprised to find that His truth isfar deeper than you thought. Once you begin to receive and believe what He really wants you to know, then you can begin to pattern your actions and choices after His ways with full confidence and an attitude of, "I'm ready—let's take it to the world, God!"

Do You Know What Your Faith Is Made Of?

Receiving, applying, and then walking in God's truth requires faith. Faith is described in the original Greek manuscripts of the Bible as trust and confidence in the goodness, power, and love of God being directed towards you. Trust is not birthed just because you say that you trust someone or something. You need to cooperate with His will and His ways to learn to trust Him. You need personal experience with His power and love to place your confidence in Him.

Faith (*trust and confidence in* the goodness and power of God) coupled with experience (*personal action taken on* a command or promise of God) can turn hope into manifested reality. Acting on your faith isn't always a physical act. It can also be a strong, purposeful rejection of anything that does not line up with God's Word—loosing all wrong patterns of thinking about an unresolved issue that you have (for example). Taking action can be a verbal binding of your will to God's will. Taking action can be a verbal loosing of your negative thoughts.

> Faith comes by hearing the Word, but faith grows by acting on and experiencing the Word.

How willing are you to test your faith? One way to do this is to determine that you are going to act as though you have already received God's answer to what you are currently praying for—the catch here is that you are going to try to act like you have already received God's perfect answer, which may not be the exact answer you had in mind. Hebrews 4:2 (NIV) tells us this:

> "*For we also have had the gospel preached to us, just as they did; but the message they heard was of no value to them, because those who heard did not combine it with faith.*"

In what areas do you find it hard to believe with full faith? Perhaps it is the salvation of a family member, your finances, a health issue, forgiveness, or something else. Find a promise in the Word of God that applies to your situation and then begin binding your will to God's will and your mind to the mind of Christ, while loosing any doubtful thoughts about whether or not God meant the promise for you. Then pray your agreement with that promise in the Word every day for at least two weeks and see what happens. Then do something that is the opposite of what your fears and your doubts have told you.

It is not really effective to bind yourself to the promises of God. That is like binding yourself to the air around you so you can breathe better. Or like binding a fish to the water so it can swim better. God's promises are all around us like air and water. They exist to be fulfilled.

If this is not happening in your life, the problem is not with the "Promisor," the problem is with the "promisees." We are the "promisees." The most effective way to pray about this is to loose all doubts, fears, and wrong patterns of thinking from your soul that would try to prevent your receipt of the promised blessing.

Practicing Your Faith

If you have been afraid to give your testimony in front of your church, bind your will to God's will and loose your *fear of man*, loose your fear of others' opinions. Don't try to hide behind saying, "I just don't want to let God down." God will be proud of any attempt you make to give Him glory. Then act upon that prayer as soon as you are able. Ask your pastor if you can testify in a Wednesday or Sunday night service, or ask your home group leader if you can share in a meeting.

If your area of struggle is that you don't feel brave enough to do anything public for God, then consider this verse, Romans 8:15 (TM):

> *"This resurrection life you received from God is not a timid, grave-tending life. It's adventurously expectant, greeting God with a childlike 'What's next, Papa?'"*

If your area of struggle is in the area of giving and tithing, then consider this verse, 2 Corinthians 9:6-8 (NIV):

> *"Remember this: Whoever sows sparingly will also reap sparingly, and whoever sows generously will also reap generously. Each man should give what he has decided in his heart to give, not reluctantly or under compulsion, for God loves a cheerful giver. And God is able to make all grace abound to you, so that in all things at all times, having all that you need, you will abound in every good work."*

You really cannot out-give God, but you need to practice giving freely to know this for yourself. If this is your struggle, pray this prayer:

Father, I bind my will to your will; I'm obligating myself to your greater plans and purposes for my life. I choose to believe the truth in your Word: whoever sows sparingly will also reap sparingly, and whoever sows generously will also reap generously. You are able to make all grace abound to me, so that I can abound in every good work. You, Lord, are the greatest giver ever—you gave your all so that I could be your child. I loose, smash, crush, and destroy all wrong patterns of thinking I have about your provision for me. I loose all fearful thinking in my mind that I won't have enough. I want to be a giver like you. Amen.

Getting Down to Ground Zero with God

It is important to know where the bottom level, basic foundation of your trust in God lies. As I was writing this book, I read a very powerful prophetic word that illustrates this point:

> *Do not be surprised when you face difficulties; it is the way of life. Rather, take every opportunity to trust Me, says the Lord, for only in troubling circumstances will you really know My mercy, favor, and grace. Rely on Me to bring you through to victory. You alone make the choice to trust and believe or to deny and deceive.*

You alone make the choice to trust and believe or to deny and deceive yourself. This is a profound truth that needs to be meditated upon every day.

It has been said that everything good that happens to you is from God; and everything bad that happens to you is from Satan. This can be very misleading to the Christian who has never learned that many things that seem bad are not and many things that seem good are not. Our perceptions of good and bad are colored by our fears, our experiences, and our level of faith. We are all going to go through some hard circumstances from

> You do not really know what you trust when you are comfortable. You find out where your trust lies when the hard times come and the bottom seems to be falling out of your life.

time to time, and they will be less frightening when we trust the One who controls them.

This would be a good thing to carve into a plaque or cross stitch on a wall hanging: God is in control of everything that happens in life—He either initiates what happens or He allows what happens.

If our lives were in the hands of a thoughtless and indifferent force, we probably would have a lot of reasons to worry. However, God is neither thoughtless nor indifferent; He is faithful, loving, and good. When you have bound your will to His will, you can hold steady in unsteady places knowing that He is present and in control. You may have to use your keys to force your soul to let Him take over its control tower.

God is never outwitted by evil, or outmaneuvered by dark forces. Therefore, as strange as it may sound to some of you, even seemingly "bad" things that happen in our lives happen with God's full knowledge and consent. This should not cause you to think you can't trust God, because you can—completely. However, everyone will experience certain things in life that happen in a world filled with sin. This is reality, and we will have to face life's harder realities at some point or another. It is really a good thing to be holding onto God's hand with complete trust at that time!

When Jesus was telling His disciples that He was going back to be with the Father, in John 16:33 (AMP), He said:

> "*I have told you these things, so that in Me you may have [perfect] peace and confidence. In the world you have tribulation and trials and distress and frustration; but be of good cheer [take courage; be confident, certain, undaunted]! For I have overcome the world.*

[I have deprived it of power to harm you and have conquered it for you.]"

Tribulations, trials, distress, and frustration in our lives do not mean that God is uncaring or out to coffee. Sometimes it means that our perspective of what is happening is wrong. For example, the digging out of a splinter in a finger can seem very bad to a child. Yet, if the splinter was not removed, it could cause an infection and even the loss of the finger. God may remove something, even a person, from your life even though it seems bad to you. His reason for doing that might be because that thing or that person would keep you from moving on in your relationship and your destiny plans with Him.

We must learn to look for God in everything that happens to us.

Unless we know how to get rid of our unsurrendered souls' old skewed thinking about what will or will not fix our brokenness, our souls will constantly try to outmaneuver God's workings in our lives. We alone make the choice to trust and believe or to deny and deceive ourselves about God's hand in everything that we face. The Keys of the Kingdom prayer principles will help you be able to accept this as a good truth.

These prayer principles will help you to make the right decisions you need to make based upon trusting Him. Pray this prayer to help yourself begin to get rid of what would hinder your trusting Him:

> **Lord, I am choosing to trust you, however I have to learn to do that. I bind my mind, will, and emotions to you, and I choose to believe that you are always with me in every circumstance I may face. I will walk through such**

times believing in your power, wisdom, and love. I refuse to be deceived by appearances and by my unsurrendered soul. I loose, smash, crush, and destroy any layers over hidden fears and unresolved issues in my life that would try to rip and tear at my trust in you. I am exposing these frightening areas to you and asking you to pour your assurance and grace into them. I loose all deceptions and works of the enemy from my life, and I thank you for your constant, faithful care of me. Amen.

Offloading Old Baggage You Don't Need

God's truth often requires you to let go of certain beliefs that you have held onto for a long time. For instance, what if, even though you had been taught that certain "evil spirits" could be cast out of you, you learned that those "spirits" were really bad attitudes in your unsurrendered soul? That could certainly require an attitude adjustment on your part.

> There are times when what we have perceived as "bad" is in reality a divine protection or correction from God working for our best.

What if you had always chosen to believe it has been your parents' fault that you have never found success in your chosen career? Then someone showed you how your own wrong choices had held you back in your career.

What adjustments would you be willing to apply to your beliefs to accept the truth that your lack of success is because you have made wrong choices? Would you be willing to force your soul to let go of its deception and its blame game? Are you willing to recognize that you have keys to use to get rid of your bad attitudes in order to make room for powerfully right ones? If you will, you can begin to recognize the good choices you can start making today.

It can be hard to embrace new truth that requires you to be accountable for negative attitudes, which have contributed to your negative circumstances. But it is the first step to becoming who God has always intended you to be.

When you can no longer just talk about the truth because the truth itself is pressing you

> Truth can be dangerous to your comfort zones. Learning God's fullness of truth can bring growing

to walk it out, things can get uncomfortable. This is because truth often requires life change. Too many Christians are content with surface truth that brings them temporary blessings or relief and allows them to stay right where they are. Our unsurrendered souls always shy away from change unless they have initiated it for self-centered reasons.

To walk in fruitfulness, we must turn away from doing things from a soul-centered point of view.

When we react out of the accumulated baggage and residue that our souls have held onto from our pasts, we can get so focused on them that we don't even consider acting on the possibilities God has placed before us. In Matthew 23:23, Jesus accused the religious scholars and Pharisees of being hopeless frauds who majored on the minor things, yet minored on the major truths of God's Word. He said they were incredibly careless about *"the meat of God's Law, things like fairness and compassion and commitment—the absolute basics!"* (TM).

Feeding on God's Word is vital to every believer. New believers need spiritual milk to grow (see 1 Peter 2:2, KJV). This is because new baby Christians are rarely able to digest the meat of the stronger scriptural truths of such things as dying to self, loving their enemies, or forgiving those who have hurt them. Such meat can choke a baby Christian, and someone will have to thump him on the back and spiritually burp him! Baby Christians need love, joy, answered prayer, guardian angels, blessings, and promises of heaven to encourage them.

The spiritually mature Christian, however, *needs and is trained by practice* to chew, swallow, and digest meat without choking as we read in Hebrews 5:13-14 (AMP):

> *"For everyone who continues to feed on milk is obviously inexperienced and unskilled in the doctrine of righteousness (of conformity to the divine will in purpose, thought, and action), for he is a mere infant [not able to talk yet]! But solid food is for full-grown men, for those whose senses and mental faculties are trained by practice to discriminate and distinguish between what is morally good and noble and what is evil and contrary either to divine or human law."*

Spoiled milk might make you sick, but spoiled meat can kill you.

The milk of the Word can be spoiled if a Christian handles it improperly and still not bring spiritual death. We have all known believers who made seriously wrong decisions based upon soulish misinterpretations of the Word, and yet they still moved on in their relationship with God. A believer, who deliberately handles spiritual meat in such a way as to spoil its true meaning, misrepresenting God's standards of holiness and twisting His truth, can cause death—spiritual and natural.

Old Mind Sets

Every believer comes to Christ with certain preformed mind sets of misinformation. When these mind sets are deeply entrenched and resistant to renewal, a believer can easily misinterpret God's Word, and thereby misinterpret God himself. Inside every one of us is a picture of God formed by what we have read, what we have been taught, what we have personally experienced, our memories, and our emotional reactions to them. Your soul will insist that it has correctly perceived this picture, but it will invariably be skewed away from His truth.

> You can actually have two pictures of God:
> 1) What you learn you should believe about Him
> 2) What you actually do believe about Him

What you learn about God has to filter down through the ideas and beliefs (right or wrong), which already exist in your mind. This fact is not always understood by Christians, lay people, or spiritual leadership. Christians have been taught for years that scripturally correct teaching should automatically clear up any wrong ideas someone might have about God. Theoretically, this is true. But experientially, scripturally correct teaching that does not fit into an unsurrendered soul's preformed mind sets can be flat out rejected!

Scriptural truth gets twisted and contaminated when it has to filter through a mind filled with old thoughts and wrong mind sets—just as pure water becomes contaminated when it is poured through a dirty filter.

God can sovereignly impart revelation knowledge into the born-again spirit any time He wants to. But usually what He speaks to the born-again spirit has to be worked through the mind, will, and emotions of the soul before it can be imparted to the world. When the soul is filled with old thoughts, wrong attitudes, and fearful memories, God's words rarely make it out through the soul to touch others in the manner He meant.

He won't storm the walls of defense that wounded, angry, fearful souls have built in order to get His message of love out to the world. He knows that we cannot be forced to show love because that would deny the very nature of love. He just patiently keeps dealing with those of us who are meant to be His hands and His voice here on earth, trying to get us to take down our walls ourselves.

> The human spirit is thrilled to shed its identity of a spiritual orphan and be united

His work of renewal in our human spirits is instantaneous when our spirits get connected to their spiritual Creator by the blood of Jesus Christ. God's work of renewal must then begin within the framework of our minds, wills, emotions, memories, experiences, and beliefs in order to begin the process of uniting our born-again spirits with our unsurrendered souls.

Our spirits are willing to allow this, but our unsurrendered souls will adamantly resist any outside interference in their status quo. They can become quite rigid and rebellious when God tries to infiltrate their strongholds with His love and truth.

It is always sad to hear Christians speak out of the rigidity of their unsurrendered souls to say, "If God wants me to give _____ up or change _____, He'll take it away, or He'll change me." Wrong! He does not change, bypass, or override our wrong beliefs. He just keeps offering His love and truth until our souls become willing to exchange old soulish beliefs and wrong ideas for His right ones.

The unsurrendered soul of the believer frequently tries to twist God's truth, tweaking His Word. God cannot allow souls to reconfigure His Word to fit their personal agendas. When God speaks, He means what He says. In Hebrews 4:12 (TM), we read:

> "God means what he says. What he says goes. His powerful Word is sharp as a surgeon's scalpel, cutting through everything, whether doubt or defense, laying us open to listen and obey."

There is also a severe warning in 2 Peter 3:16 (AMP) about twisting the Scriptures to fit your own agendas and misconceptions:

> "There are some things in those [epistles of Paul] that are difficult to understand, which the ignorant and unstable twist and misconstrue to their own utter destruction, just as [they distort and misinterpret] the rest of the Scriptures."

Old Testament warnings about twisting the counsel of God's Word are found in Isaiah 5:24 (NKJV):

> "As the fire devours the stubble, and the flame consumes the chaff, so their root will be as rottenness, and their blossom will ascend like dust; because they have rejected the law of the LORD of hosts, and despised the word of the Holy One of Israel."

When truth is forsaken, errors multiply. When truth is cherished, we are healed and shaped into God's plans and purposes for our lives. Both your unsurrendered soul and Satan will try to convince you that a little "harmless error" might work best in the overall picture of things. Only a constant washing in the Word of God can keep you from such deceptions.

God expects us to believe His Word and then act accordingly. We must stop deceiving ourselves that if we really do "mean well" when we bend His Word just a bit, then God will agreeably allow us to pursue our "good intentions."

We must never rationalize our so-called "good intentions" as an excuse to twist or tweak the truth of God's Word.

For example: "I am only cutting a small corner in my business dealings (or in my personal finances), but I know it will be okay because it will give me more money to do something for God." Or this lie for example: "I know I shouldn't repeat this, but I'm only telling it to you so you can pray for her." Any of your thoughts or words that begin with "I probably shouldn't …" or "I'm just trying to …" should probably be loosed immediately.

Acting Upon Your Hope

God has said,

> "I know the plans I have for you . . . plans to prosper you and not to harm you, plans to give you hope and a future" (Jeremiah 29:11, NIV).

This Scripture holds the promise of being prospered, of having hope, and facing a future filled with God's good plans. How could anyone resist that? It is resisted every day by those who are afraid to believe it (believers and non-believers alike), those who base their understanding of God upon the filter of the negative experiences of their lives.

It is time to get down to the basics of changing and impacting lives for God—your life and other lives—believers and unbelievers. It is time to begin bearing fruit for His Kingdom! Jesus said in Matthew 16:19 (KJV):

> "*I will give unto thee the keys of the kingdom of heaven: and whatsoever thou shalt bind on earth shall be bound in heaven: and whatsoever thou shalt loose on earth shall be loosed in heaven.*"

As previously stated, Christ's giving of these keys in the first part of this verse represents the giving of permission, authority, and ability to enter into the kingdom of heaven to transact spiritual business. The remainder of the verse tells the believer how to transact that spiritual business. In Isaiah 22:22 the prophet Isaiah described a time when Eliakim would be elevated as the king's steward, he would be given a key to the entire palace, and he would have authority to act in the king's name. In Matthew 16:19, we have given the Keys of the Kingdom with authority to act in our King's name.

The question is: How are we going to use that power and authority?

Summary

1. Beyond your shattered strongholds is where you begin to produce the most important thing you will ever produce in your Christian walk: FRUIT FOR THE KINGDOM OF GOD!

2. God desires that we would influence those who are in the world at this time, finishing the works that Jesus left for us to do after He went to be with His Father.

3. Jesus Christ has given supernatural keys of power and authority to His believers to enable all of us to surrender to the good plans and great blessings of God.

4. Acquiring a renewed mind is a process of spending time in the Word, prayer and communion with God, the application of good spiritual teachings, and loosing wrong patterns of thinking and wrong beliefs to receive His thoughts.

5. If your soul is filled with old fears and bad memories, it is not easy to trust God to give you His deeper truths in stages you can handle.

6. It is important to know where the ground level, bottom line, basic foundation of your trust in God lies.

7. You alone make the choice to trust and believe God or to deny and deceive yourself.

8. Unless we know how to get rid of our unsurrendered souls' old skewed thinking about what will or will not fix our brokenness, our unsurrendered souls will constantly try to outmaneuver God's workings in our lives.

9. To fully receive God's truth, you will need to let go of wrong beliefs that you have held onto for a long time.

10. To walk in fruitfulness, we must turn away from doing things from a soul-centered point of view.

11. What you learn about God has to filter down through the ideas and beliefs (right or wrong) that already exist in your mind.

12. When truth is forsaken, errors multiply. When truth is cherished, we are healed and shaped into God's plans and purposes for our lives.

Chapter 2

Strongholds Shut Out the Truth

The Revelation Grows

When I wrote the original *Shattering Your Strongholds*, I remember talking to someone about naming the book *All You Ever Wanted To Know About Binding and Loosing*. I look back at that now and think about how little I really knew about this new revelation at that time, yet how powerful it still was. I had managed to grasp the most basic truths of using the Keys of the Kingdom, but I had no idea how much more would come.

I had so many questions when I was newly saved. Should I do this? Should I do that? Why did this happen? How can I get that to happen? What DOES God want of me?

I didn't bother to ask these questions of God very often, because I never seemed to hear Him say anything back to me. I had no clue that this was because I had only opened the lines of my understanding to receive the answers I wanted to hear. I had asked Jesus Christ to be my Lord and Master, but I had no idea how that was supposed to play out in my daily life.

I quickly learned one thing, however: When you accepted Jesus Christ as your Lord and Master, the Holy Spirit seemed to think He had been given the green light to start sorting out the pieces of your life. When this happened, my soul started screaming, "Out of control! Out of control!" I didn't realize it, but my soul was the Extreme Control Freak of all times.

I remember fearing that if I gave God too much control in my life, He would make me do things I didn't want to do. I went through my "Salvation Army street ministry phase" where I was sure He would make me wear a long black dress and a black bonnet while standing on a street corner with a tin cup and a tambourine if I didn't watch Him very carefully. I was still in the formative years of my relationship with Him where I thought I was still calling the shots.

Then I went through my "having to go to deepest, darkest Africa and live in a small hut phase" where I just knew God would make me roll bandages all day for the missionary hospital. Neither of these things came to pass in my life, but I was sure at the time that it was only because I had kept my eyes on God so He couldn't make any moves I hadn't approved.

> There is a purpose and an order to the arranging of the pieces of our lives that requires certain pieces to be in place first.

I actually had no idea what God had in mind for my life; I was afraid that it would be tedious, hard, and boring. Then a few new things began to come into my life. I joined the church choir; I went to work for my senior pastor; and I began to do some ghost writing. I even found a few heroines in the ministry that I decided I wanted to be like: Iverna Tompkins, Roxanne Brant, and Hattie Hammond. I was not aware of it at the time, but I was learning to belong, to love, and to be loved.

I also had a major relationship rift with my father after becoming a Christian, and the church choir became my surrogate family at that time. I was not yet able to discern the hand of God at work around me, but I now know He surrounded me with friends and spiritual mother and father figures in those early years. I felt I had a family to belong to, which was very important to me at that time.

After a few years, I reached a point where the remaining wrong things of my life that I was still clinging to were beginning to choke me: unforgiveness, unresolved issues, anger, and I'm sure a few other things I don't remember now. For a season, I couldn't seem to find anything of God at all.

Only when everything I was trying to do crumbled to dust did I finally began to spend serious time on my knees. I prayed, "God, do whatever you have to. Crush me, break me, mold me, and make me willing. I don't care what you have to do, God, just get it over with. I don't want to go on this way." The Holy Spirit was faithful and some of the things that came out of those prayers were pretty hard to cooperate with. But as God began answering, my life began to change dramatically.

I began to search the Word to see if what I had been taught was true. This was not easy since I was like a

> Christians often concentrate so intensely on a single facet they've been taught to believe, they miss the bigger picture of God's Word and works completely.

spiritual baby bird whose parent always pre-digested whatever it was supposed to eat. I loved letting the pastors and the visiting speakers feed me pre-digested truth. Yet, something kept nudging me to begin trying to find my own truth, and I began to find some amazing gaps in my understanding.

I realized that I was only scratching the surface of my Christianity.

At that time, I was just a born-again "Christian" in name only. I did not yet have a real relationship with God that I could recognize as anything other than the Bible said that He loved me and I should obey Him.

Back to the Beginning

I finally settled my relationship with the Lord in Sacramento, California, in the spring of 1972. As I said in the original *Shattering Your Strongholds*, my early views of Christianity ran parallel to the Burger King jingle that promised I could "have it my way." I believed God was waiting to take my order, charge it to Jesus' account, and deliver the goodies with a minimum amount of standing in line on my part.

I pursued my anemic relationship with God the hard way, because I was spiritually malnourished most of the time. I only nibbled on teachings that I liked, and I turned up my nose at anything tasting too strong or that chewed too hard. Fortunately, I attended a strong church that also sustained an excellent Bible school. There was so much meat flowing over the pulpit in that church, even the most carnal Christians grew in spite of themselves!

> Truth is not what you believe just because your most spiritual friend or your favorite evangelist says it is so.

Comfortable as I was for awhile, eventually I began to feel the need to learn for myself what was and what wasn't true in my own beliefs. You can just keep walking along with the Christian crowd and hoping you are going in the right direction, but you are going to have to get serious at some point about where you might end up when you get there.

You begin to realize that you can't just memorize the Word and expect it to be working in your life with signs and wonders following. You begin to realize that you can't just blindly swallow whatever truth you hear from the pulpit without applying it in your own life. You can say you believe a truth, but you finally learn that you have to *experience that truth* for yourself before it's ever going to set you free. Jesus said (John 8:31-32, KJV):

> *"If ye continue in my word, then are ye my disciples indeed; and ye shall **know** the truth, and the truth shall make you free."*

Knowing the Truth

Your unsurrendered soul does not like the taste or even the smell of anything God puts forth to encourage you, let alone the strongest taste of all: the taste of truth. This is because His truth is always seasoned and flavored with obedience and surrender. The truth about truth is that you have very little understanding of what it really is all about until you taste it and obey it.

In the original Greek text, one of the meanings for truth is "having nothing concealed." You have to handle and act upon truth to see what may yet be concealed from your understanding of it. This doesn't automatically happen by just attending the biggest seminars, viewing the latest videos, and reading the newest books. Wisdom comes from experiencing truth. Ephesians 3:19 (AMP) says:

"That you may really come to know—practically, through experience for yourselves—the love of Christ, which far surpasses mere knowledge without experience."

These prayer keys in themselves are only a means to an end, but they must be used with some diligence to keep your unsurrendered soul from playing possum on you. The phrase "playing possum" first found its way into print in the 1820s, meaning to beat around the bush and evade the truth. The possum (the only marsupial in North America) is a one-of-a-kind animal that has survived for some rather interesting reasons:

1. It will eat almost anything, including garbage can scraps.
2. It puts up a great pretense of being ferocious to cause some would-be attackers to back off—but it is all a bluff.
3. It has claws and a prehensile tail that allow it to quickly climb a tree to avoid confrontation.
4. It has the ability to "play" dead, which makes it unappealing to many predators that prefer their meals kicking and squealing.
5. It squirts a foul smelling liquid when it feels threatened, usually right before its launches its "dead" act routine.

This really ugly little guy (looks like a fat rat the size of a cat with little scrawny legs, a long snout, big naked ears, and a long naked tail) reminds me a lot of the unsurrendered soul:

1. It will swallow almost anything that intrigues its less than godly interests, seems to satisfy its curiosity, or supports its wrong beliefs.

2. It often puts up a great pretense of being quite ferocious to get people to back off.
3. It will climb anything or get under anything to avoid a confrontation over its tacky ways.
4. It has the ability to play dead (also dumb and dumber) when it is backed into a corner and feels trapped.
5. It can squirt out all kinds of foul attitudes and nasty remarks when it feels threatened.

Anybody up for a possum hunt?

Understanding Self-Erected Strongholds

The born-again believer can love the Lord and still have an unsurrendered soul—a carnal, worldly, sinful mind; an enforcer-mentality type of self-will; and a set of raggedy, reactive emotions. The believer's mind does not automatically get renewed at the moment of salvation. Most minds come into the state of salvation filled with old attitudes, worldly patterns of thinking, and some pretty strange ideas.

That would not seem too difficult to rectify when the new believer so strongly feels the love of Jesus Christ. Unfortunately, many of the soul's old ideas and bad attitudes are aggressively protected by the soul's self-erected strongholds in spite of the divine love felt.

The key to receiving renewal as fast as possible is to tear down the strongholds protecting all of the old patterns of wrong thinking and deceptions. Unfortunately, some Christians never accomplish this; instead, they may spend their entire lives trying to override God's truth with their preconceived ideas and misconceptions of who He is and what He wants of them. This is sin clothed in self-deception. Romans 8:7 (NIV) says this:

"The sinful mind is hostile to God. It does not submit to God's law, nor can it do so."

It is sad when Christians have formed their concept of God from pre-salvation ideas and personal experiences rather than the truth He has revealed about himself in His Word. Our souls' unresolved issues couldn't care less about truth and may even begin to hiss and spit when we offer it to them. We can trace such emotionally negative reactions back to unresolved issues in our lives. We usually have incredibly strong walls built around those scary questions.

Many believers also react out of old mind sets about their unresolved issues when they stumble and fall in their walk with God. They know that the Word says He loves them, yet they still fear He will angrily turn away when they don't live up to His expectations. After all, isn't that what Mom (Dad, Grampa, Aunt Mona, etc.) did? Or they believe He will say, "You're just not good enough to be this close to me; now go sit in the back where I can't see you."

> No matter how discouraged you might be right now, you can be free of the old mind sets and distortions in your understanding from your past's baggage.

Such deceptions and misconceptions do not come from God—they come from old mind sets in these believers' souls that disable their ability to believe what God has written about himself. Unfortunately, those wrong mind sets are fiercely protected by strongholds. Too often Christians are instructed to just change their minds and to let go of their wrong beliefs, without ever being taught how to actually do that. Pray this prayer to start the demolition process of your strongholds that are preventing you from cleaning house in your soul:

Lord, I bind my will to your will. I'm so tired of trying to keep it under control. Please teach it how to become yoked with your plans and purposes. I do not want my soul to be able to establish any more hiding places for its wrong beliefs and bad attitudes. I do not want my soul to be able to justify and rationalize its deception any longer. I do not want my mind looking for ways to rephrase its fear and its anger, so I am choosing now to obligate and bind my will to you and my mind to the mind of Christ. I loose, smash, crush, and destroy all of my stronghold thinking and the strongholds already built. I choose to tear apart all forms of defensiveness and denial in my soul. I want to be fully surrendered and open to you. Amen.

The New Creature Process

It is sad that so many Christians today continue to see themselves in terms of their upbringing, their shattered marriages, their lost jobs, their lack of money, etc., rather than their potential in Christ. This negative way of looking at things is a hard way to live—but in many cases, the Christian stubbornly refuses to believe he or she could be any other way. Titus 3:5 (NIV) says this:

> Some people insist upon seeing themselves only as the product of their pasts.

> "He saved us, not because of righteous things we had done, but because of his mercy. He saved us through the washing of rebirth and renewal by the Holy Spirit."

Many have experienced the refreshing bathing of the rebirth, but they still hold on tight to their old beliefs and old ways just in case the working out of the renewal is delayed. "Never hurts to have an ace in the hole, does it?" your soul growls.

The Bible clearly states that when you are saved, you are a new creature—free of the guilt and punishment of your past sins (2 Corinthians 5:17). But accepting this truth involves a process that must take place before it can be settled in your soul.

New ways of thinking come about by the washing of the Word. New feelings come about through the healing balance of the Holy Spirit. You learn to realize that truth must be tested and experienced, and your old ways of thinking and reacting must be loosed and turned away from. Deception and denial must be exposed and tossed out. Your experience with embracing God's good things and rejecting your soul's shabby, ratty things will bring you through the process of transitioning into your new creature status.

As believers, we are walking around in tents of flesh that are pretty used to being in agreement with our unsurrendered souls/old natures. Suddenly into this murky partnership, a new entity has shown up: born-again spirits indwelt by the Spirit of God. What a dichotomy! Your old nature is confronted with a new nature in your life, the nature of Christ that needs to be in charge. This scene can cause your soul to react and respond rather viciously.

> As your new spiritual nature begins to grow in you, the trouble begins.

It will throw up anything it can to stop you from following the leading of the nature of Christ within you. It will try sickness, depression, fear, insecurity, terror in the night—anything it can throw at you to distract you from your relationship with God. It is no wonder that we as Christians can feel totally undone at times.

First John 3:8 tells us that the reason the Son of God appeared on earth was to destroy the devil's works. Jesus then left full provision for us to do the same thing. All we need to do to appropriate that provision is get rid of the rubble in our lives and close the open doors in our souls. This is God's decree and His will for us. Your will must choose to call your life on earth into alignment and agreement with God's will in heaven. God will not force you to do this, but He will help you just as it says in Philippians 2:13 (AMP) which gives His plan:

> *"It is God Who is all the while effectually at work in you—energizing and creating in you the power and desire—both to will and to work for His good pleasure and satisfaction and delight."*

Why Are You and I Here?

God did not make you just so He would have someone to carry out His wishes and do His work here on earth. Surprise! He has angels to do that for Him. God made us so He would have lots of children to inherit His Family Business. He is the one who originated the Take Your Son or Daughter to Work With You Days.

God made you with a unique potential to bring joy and pleasure to Him in a way no

Every one of us knows at least one special person who can lift our hearts and bring a smile to our faces just by coming near to us. You were created with the potential to do that same thing by throwing yourself into cooperating with God with your only motive being that you just love going to work with your Father.

After many years of bumbling and grumbling around in my own willfulness, I began to think that maybe there was a heavenly reason that I had been born into this time. Maybe

There are too few believers today who are willing to endure the time spent, energy expended, and the stretching required to experience the opening up of His multi-faceted truths.

all of the other Christians weren't the only ones He was going to use after all! Once I caught that bit of truth, the Lord began to show me that I needed to spend more time with Him to learn the many facets of His truths. He wanted to turn my single-level surface understanding into real spiritual understanding.

Sadly, many do not want any more than single-level surface understanding. They are like the person who says, "I'm comfortable with what I already believe. Don't try to confuse me with facts."

God's truth, when opened up to reveal more than its surface layer, can show you the reality of soulish situations that you could misinterpret otherwise. Personal agendas which are hidden to the natural mind can be revealed to you. As you pray the binding and loosing prayers, you will find that many things begin to come into focus once your soul is hindered from distracting you in its flailing around trying to protect its own personal agendas.

Interpreting Christianese and Personal Agendas

It is hard to see what lies behind the facial expressions and concerned words of others when your discernment is being scrambled with urgent drives coming up out of your unmet needs and unhealed hurts. Carnal motives can be presented in lovely "Christianese," the language of the unsurrendered souls in many believers. This religious language can be interpreted for what it is by God's spiritual revelation getting through to any soul that is in the process of trying to clear out its rubble so it can hear Him speak.

Christianese: "I'm only telling you this secret about George so you can pray for him to succeed in this new leadership role. I'm praying that he will." **Hidden truth:** "I hope you will pass this on to the pastor so that I can have a chance to get that role."

Christianese: "I really admire Carla so much for having overcome her drinking problem. I pray all the time that she won't slip back into those old patterns when she's under the stress as she is now—oh, I'm sorry. I really shouldn't have said that." **Hidden truth:** "I'm sick of everybody in this group thinking Carla is so good, because I know it would only take one difficult thing to put her back over the edge."

Christianese: "Don't you think someone should tell the pastor about the problems that Jack and Betty are having? I mean, shouldn't the pastor know that they really aren't ready to lead that seminar on relationships? I'm not brave enough to tell him, but it would be good if somebody was." **Hidden truth:** "I don't want to be the one who tells the pastor to get rid of them, but maybe I can convince you to do it. I wanted to lead that seminar myself."

All new believers come into the body of Christ with personal agendas and motives. This is a fact of human nature. They need to learn how to shed these trappings of their human natures (USPPP: Unsurrendered Souls Pushing Personal Plans) to

> As you make room your soul for all of God's truth, you can begin to "read between the lines" of situations and become a blessing to others.

make room for their new creature natures (SSTGP: Souls Surrendered To God's Plans).

When you allow God to both expand His love in your soul as well as reveal the hidden layers of truth in those who are still operating out of their unsurrendered souls, you can become a part of God's solutions instead of being part of His problems.

Being part of God's solution requires you to begin to empty out your unsurrendered soul's fears or doubts about getting involved with other people. You cannot bear fruit for the Kingdom of God from an ivory tower. You have to come down out of your safety zone and mingle with the rest of the crowd to influence them for good.

Sitting up in your ivory tower religiously reading your Bible will never be enough for you to be a part of the solution either. In John 5, Jesus acknowledged the religious Jews had studied the Scriptures and searched them diligently, believing their answer to eternal life lay in the words. Yet, they were missing everything they were supposed to learn from them—the overwhelming abundance of truth and life in Jesus Christ that needed to be shared with the world. We read in John 5:39-40, (AMP):

> *"You search and investigate and pore over the Scriptures diligently, because you suppose and trust that you have eternal life through them. And these (very Scriptures) testify about Me! And you still are not willing (but refuse) to come to Me, so that you might have life."*

Moving past just reading the Word without ever actually working it out, without experiencing it in your life is like reading about how to sing without ever hearing anyone sing. Such a written teaching may be quite accurate, yet it is only a collection of words until you try to actually open your mouth and learn to put different tones to your voice.

> It is much harder for the enemy to take something from you that you have a personal experience with.

This is the same as applying what you read in the Word. You must read the Word and then put thought and action to it. Many life-giving concepts in the Word become unshakable, powerful, personal truths you will always be able to stand upon once you have turned them into personal experience.

Think about how you learned what the word "hot" meant. After a few times of burning yourself, it would become increasingly difficult for anyone to get you to put your hands back on that oven door. This is pretty unshakable knowledge gained from your personal experience. You need to apply the same principle to understanding Scripture.

God's Word is not to be cherished as a good-luck charm (using it in prayer only when you want God's extra help with something) or to soothe a disturbed mind by bringing temporary relief from anxiety (using it like a sedative to calm your nerves). Better than extra help or calming sedatives, the true blessings of the Word of God are found in the fact that it was given to us to use so that our lives would always be filled with His presence and His love wherever we walk. Not only in this life—but forever.

The personal application of a truth from the Word tests and proves your faith in what God has said would come from obeying His commands. Faith does indeed come by hearing the Word, but faith only grows by experiencing the Word.

Faith and experience turn hope into manifested reality. When you act on what you read in the Word in the natural realm of your influence, you will begin to interact with divine purposes in the spiritual realm.

Three-In-One Creative Harmony or Chaos: Spirit, Soul, and Body

Your born-again spirit has a direct communion with God's Spirit—it is no longer a spiritual orphan. Try to imagine how your orphaned spirit felt when it was in submission to your unsurrendered soul's plans and purposes before you were saved, having no link to its Father. Once your spirit became united with the Father, it only wanted to be closer to and in deeper relationship with Him.

> God has never desired that we all be perfect little cookie-cutter Christians.

Your soul consists of three parts, which make you completely unique: your mind, your will, and your emotions. The composite makeup of your experiences, your relationships, your learning processes, and your opinions and beliefs makes you different from anyone else in the world. God has designed each of us to be that way. He is not desiring that you be a perfect example of a model Christian like every other "perfect model Christian." (What is that, anyway?) He wants you to express yourself to others in the world through your own personal, unique ability to share His love. No one else on earth can do that just as you can.

If you don't get rid of your soul's religious beliefs, it may try to get you to copy other Christian's methods of walking out their faith. While that may be the way to first learn how to pray, walk, and respond as a Christian, you must transition out of that mode. God has some very distinctive things He wants to teach you about becoming fruitful for His Kingdom purposes. He has many unique styles of showing love and compassion that He wants to work through each one of us.

Don't worry that He might ever run out of individual styles before He gets to you. If He could create thousands of species of unique animals and thousands of species of unique plant forms (all with their own DNA structures), He can create some pretty spectacular styles of being fruitful just for you and for me.

Your body is in touch with the earthly things of the world around you, receiving and responding to its environment through its senses of sight, sound, smell, taste, and touch.

> Your body is a follower, a reactor, and a vehicle that needs to be in agreement with some part of you.

While your body can react to urges and directives from your soul, it has no ability to make intellectual, emotional, or spiritual decisions on its own. It just waddles after whoever seems to be setting the pace at the time.

If your unsurrendered soul is the big kid on your block, your body will agree with and conform to its desires and directives. If you have stripped your soul of all of its personal agendas and drives through the binding and loosing prayers, then your born-again spirit will assume the role of leadership on the block. Your body will then begin to conform to your born-again spirit's desires, directives, and revelation input from God.

Your spirit, soul, and body are together a fearfully and wonderfully made creation of God. Yet at times these same three divinely-created parts of your being seem to keep running into each other like the old Keystone Kops slapstick movies! The chaotic struggle among these three parts of your being is not how God intended His design for your life to be played out. He has a much bigger and better plan.

Imagine for a moment that you are a really big NBA basketball fan. This coming Sunday morning the final playoff game between your favorite basketball team and its biggest rival is going to be played. This is a game that is being touted as the Game of the Decade! You wake up Sunday morning and your born-again spirit says, "Oh happy day! Oh happy day! We're going to church to worship the Lord and talk about Jesus!"

Your soul snaps to attention and immediately begins to rationalize another plan: "But the biggest game ever is going to be played this morning and the TiVo isn't working. I can't miss that game! We go to church all the time, so just missing one Sunday morning isn't going to kill us. I know, I'll go to church tonight and next Wednesday, too! That will make up for missing this morning."

Then your body chimes in, "Whatever! Let's just go to the Pancake Palace and have a big yummy breakfast first!"

Our self-indulgent bodies, unsurrendered souls, and born-again spirits constantly have different agendas they are trying to push. That is when the civil war inside each one of us can heat up and things get really confusing unless you know how to clear the playing field! Your born-again spirit should always be the point-guard on the basketball court (or the quarterback on the football field, or the captain of the rowing team). That is because your born-again spirit always has a direct line to the Master Coach's instructions. Learn to cooperate with it so it can implement the Master Coach's instructions in your life.

Breaking It Down Further

Your mind is constantly gathering information from the world around you, receiving or rejecting input according to what your soul has preprogrammed it to receive. For example, if your soul has stored painful memories of people betraying you, then it will program your mind to be suspicious of anyone asking you to trust him or her.

Your soul influences your ability to receive new understanding, and it will strongly influence any input that it feels must be rejected. Your mind first analyzes input to see if it matches the acceptable criteria of the soul, and then it will come to various conclusions. These conclusions are influenced by what your natural senses (sight, sound, smell, taste, and touch) have perceived to be true. Unfortunately, your natural senses can be completely deceived. Think about some of the mind-bending optical illusions you've seen.

Your emotions kick in to see if your mind's conclusions are going to press any of their hot buttons: fear, anger, stress, reactions, etc. Emotions can enhance your life or nearly destroy it. They can add delicious flavor to your life, or when they are allowed to pour forth in huge amounts, they can overpower and ruin everything you experience. Just imagine the difference in an apple pie made with half a teaspoon of nutmeg compared to an apple pie made with half a pound of nutmeg.

Filled with sensory perception (Did I really see what I think I just saw?) and emotional flavoring (This is making me really nervous!), your mind's conclusions are then downloaded to your will for some form of action—fight, flight, fidget, or file for later action. Your will is the enforcer of your soul. Your mind conceives an idea, the emotions check it out to see what feelings it might stir up, and then the will uses its drive (boldness, courage, stubbornness) to enact any action it considers to be appropriate. Sometimes your will authorizes a reaction quite the opposite of what your born-again spirit would advise.

> Reactions out of your unsurrendered soul to what you believe you are perceiving almost always cause you to make wrong choices.

For example, if you have never overcome old patterns of reacting to irrational anger heaped on you as a child, your "fight or flight" response to anger may cause you to act irrationally. Angry words, stressful facial expressions, and tension in the air can cause frightening emotional memories to pump fear into your mind.

Your will can quickly analyze this mental and emotional download as a message to become confrontational and aggressive, or the messages surging over all your circuits can be interpreted as a command to get out of Dodge City! The "fidget or file" responses are generally not quite so dramatic. But if your soul had been surrendered to the will of God, you could have waited to see what God wanted to do in you or through you.

In order to heal you of irrational feelings and wrong beliefs, God will allow difficult situations to happen in your life to reveal your need for healing and to convince you that you cannot heal yourself. It is a far more powerful learning experience for you to recognize when God has just shown himself strong on your behalf in a difficult situation than it is for you to hear the pastor say that He will do that for you.

To respond wisely to your circumstances, your mind, will, and emotions need to be submitted to the will of God and the mind of Christ to override erroneous input from your natural senses that could influence wrong choices. The best choice you ever made was to accept

> Wrong choices may slow down your spiritual progress because of their consequences, but if you repent and allow the Holy Spirit to teach you by them, you will move forward again.

Jesus Christ as your Savior. Every other choice that you make from that point on, even the wrong ones, will ultimately be worked together for good when you are one of those who love God and are called according to His purposes (Romans 8:28).

Regardless of what anyone tells you, God's great plans and purposes for your life are not diminished or reduced because you have messed up. They are not even diminished if you've messed up twenty-six times! He doesn't want you to go through the embarrassment, pain, and guilt that you feel when you fail, but He won't take your future away from you if you do. He will lovingly try to teach you how not to make the same mistake again.

Your life from this day on, including your relationship with the Lord and with others, will only be diminished by your unfounded fears that you have worn out God's patience, grace, and mercy with you. Your life will be greatly enhanced if you begin to believe these last two paragraphs!

Your Enemy Loves Your Strongholds

While your unsurrendered soul keeps trying to trip up your attempts to step out on God's promises, it is not the only entity working to trip you up. Satan will also wage war against your attempts to get in on God's plans. He knows a lot about you (he's very nosy and he keeps massive records), and he will use that knowledge to attack you in a manner that will upset you the most. Unchallenged strongholds give him room, footholds, and opportunities to really mess with your head.

So, what do you do if you don't know if it is your unsurrendered soul or Satan causing your distress? Pray the binding and loosing prayers. Bind your will to God's will, your mind to Christ's mind, and your emotions to the healing balance of the Holy Spirit. Loose, smash, crush, and destroy all strongholds in your unsurrendered soul. Loose the enemy's works that he has set against you. That will pretty well cover both of those rascals!

Don't ever forget that Satan is not afraid of you. Don't believe the songs we've all sung in church about him that say, "... he's under my feet, he's under my feet," and so on. If he were under your feet, he wouldn't be able to continue making your life so difficult. He is extremely intelligent; he has untold numbers of spirits to help him; and he is a master of deception.

> Satan knows that your fears, deceptions, and the strongholds protecting them have been tearing up your peace since you were born.

He does not put forth his deceptions and lies, his attacks on truth, in shades of black. He moves about in shades of palest grey that always deceive those who try to deal with him in the natural realm. He uses your soul's strongholds to weasel deception and confusion into your mind, will, and emotions. His plans against you are designed to take you down through your own soul's fear and doubt.

The original Greek word for "stronghold" is *ochuroma*, which basically means to fortify something by holding it safely. To paraphrase *Thayer's Greek-English Lexicon of the New*

Testament, a stronghold is what one uses to strengthen and defend a personal belief, idea, or opinion against any outside opposition. We "build" strongholds to *fortify and protect and defend* what we have chosen to believe about ourselves, about others, about Satan, and about God.

When we are determined that we are right, our souls will happily keep rationalizing, justifying, and defending our right to keep believing that we are right.

One example of building a stronghold is something that happened many years ago when I was hurt by something I learned a pastor had said about me. I actually heard this while I was in the middle of reading the very straightforward commandment of Ephesians 4:26-27 (TM). I believe my finding out about the pastor's words at that precise moment was established by God to work these verses out in my life:

> *"Go ahead and be angry. You do well to be angry—but don't use your anger as fuel for revenge. And don't stay angry. Don't go to bed angry. Don't give the Devil that kind of foothold in your life."*

These verses are a very clear command to deal with our anger as quickly as possible because unrighteous anger (about 99.99 percent of all your anger and mine) tears up your soul, your health, and your relationships—not to mention that unsurrendered anger gives the enemy added opportunities to hurt you even more. But I was angry and I was determined to confront this pastor. I was in complete denial of the truth I had just been studying in the Word. In the *Amplified Bible*, Ephesians 4:26-27 is translated this way:

> *"When angry, do not sin; do not ever let your wrath (your exasperation, your fury or indignation) last until*

*the sun goes down. Leave no [such] room or foothold
for the devil, [give no opportunity to him]."*

There is nothing in either one of these versions that says it is
okay to be angry if it is a family member who has betrayed
you, or that it is okay to be mad if a minister of God has spoken
wrong words about you, or even that it is okay to remain
angry if you have been abused in a terrible manner. Note:
There is NO sliding scale of abuse here that eventually says,
"It's okay to get mad and stay angry as long as your offense
is at the high end of this scale."

I kept hearing a small voice in my head saying, "Don't do it,
don't do it—remember what you just read in the Bible" as I
set out to find this pastor. Each time the Scripture came back
to my mind, I rationalized that this was not just anyone who
had spoken mean words about me; it was a pastor—a man of
God! Aha! I justified my anger by thinking that he above all
other people should have known better. I defended my right
to be angry with him by rationalizing that he was not being
a good minister.

In other words, I had allowed my soul to effectively transfer
the blame of my disobedience to him—my disobedience was
now the pastor's fault! This is a sly trick the enemy loves to
promote. Then I began to even deny that I was personally
angry, insisting instead that I just wanted to see God's justice
served.

I set off to carry out my mission of "godly" justice and my
car died right in the middle of downtown Sacramento on
Labor Day at 5:45 p.m. in at least 108 degrees heat. I ended up
having to pay a small fortune to have my car towed because
the tow trucks went on holiday time at 5:30 p.m. Then I had
to pay to have my car locked in a mechanic's yard over the

whole three-day weekend because everyone was off for the holiday. I was grounded for three days, which was only the beginning of the amount of time it took for me to begin to finally listen to God.

Before this whole scenario was over, several more serious things came out of my bad attitude and wrong reaction all because I had given the devil a foothold and an opportunity to mess in my life when I deliberately refused to obey God. The stronghold I built was not a stronghold of anger; it was a stronghold built to defend my right to stay angry in spite of God's Word telling me to deal with it and go to bed with a clear conscience.

The worst sin of all is not that I refused to obey God, but that I tried to justify and excuse my disobedience. When you disobey God, DON'T try to make excuses to Him—drop to your knees and repent, asking Him to forgive you. Ask Him to help you deal with your feelings towards anyone else who is involved, and to help you get rid of your bad attitude and anger. Then begin to cooperate—doing your part—with your request by loosing your wrong feelings and attitudes.

I don't always get it right as quickly as I wish, but I am faster now in realizing that defending my right to be angry is definitely not smart! I try very hard to let go of any anger or hard feelings that might arise, and especially to let them go before the sun goes down. I don't want to cooperate with the devil getting any footholds in my life.

Those Awful UN Words

When your soul chooses to believe a lie, it will fight to protect its wrong belief. The lie might be that you are unloved, unwanted, unnecessary, unsuccessful, unworthy, or any of those other ugly "UN" words." Your soul will then build a stronghold to protect this lie by rationalizing why it is true. Attempts by others to convince you that you are wrong are viewed by your soul as attacks on your intelligence and your integrity, causing it to reinforce the stronghold even more.

Once you decide a lie must be true, your soul will go to great lengths to defend your right to believe it.

Satan knows this and loves it. Strongholds open up opportunities for him to further his deceptions and to manipulate you through them. He was defeated by Christ at the cross over 2000 years ago, but he is still very smart. Even though Satan made a deadly error of judgment when he challenged God and was cast out of heaven, he is still far more cunning than any of us. He is also very dangerous if he manages to deceive you. Satan has no power over you unless you give him room, opportunities, and footholds in your life. Strongholds give him those footholds because they are built to rationalize and excuse sin.

When you refuse to tear down strongholds around your wrong beliefs and misconceptions about having the right to remain at odds with others who have walked through your life, Satan will jump on those opportunities like steel on a magnet.

Satan cannot read your mind, but he has kept exquisite records of your life and will use them against you every time you give him an opportunity.

He will harass you and reinforce your hurt and your guilt, as well as your fear of having your sins exposed. Satan does not have to read your mind; he simply has to set up a replay of the circumstances that caused your neediness, your questions, or your pain, and then watch how you react. If you panic or get angry, then he knows that is still a hot button to push. If you walk right by his replay without so much as flinching, he dead files that button.

The choice to use the Keys of the Kingdom prayer principles is yours. You don't have to wonder whether or not it will work, just try it and you'll see for yourself. You can apply pressure to any deception or error in your soul if you will try this way of praying. If your beliefs are not true, then they will have to go when you pray this way. If your beliefs are right and true, they will stand. Is that not a win-win situation?

What if there really is something new and powerful that you can learn about binding and loosing prayers? Do you want to miss out?

Summary

1. You have to handle and act upon truth to see what may yet be concealed from your understanding of it.
2. Wisdom comes from truth found and then acted upon—truth experienced.
3. The born-again believer can love the Lord and still have an unsurrendered soul—a carnal, worldly, sinful mind; an enforcer-mentality type of self-will; and a set of raggedy and reactive emotions.
4. The key to receiving renewal as fast as possible is to tear down the strongholds protecting all of the old patterns of wrong thinking and deceptions.
5. Your will must choose to call your life on earth into alignment and agreement with God's will in heaven.

6. God's truth, when opened up to reveal more than its surface layer, can show you the reality of soulish situations that you could misinterpret otherwise.

7. When you act on what you read in the Word in the natural realm of your influence, you will begin to interact with divine purposes in the spiritual realm.

8. Your mind is constantly gathering information from the world around you, receiving or rejecting input according to what your soul has preprogrammed it to receive.

9. In order to heal you of irrational feelings and wrong beliefs, God will allow difficult situations to happen in your life to reveal your need for healing and to convince you that you cannot heal yourself.

10. Regardless of what anyone tells you, God's great plans and purposes for your life are not diminished or reduced because you have messed up.

11. We "build" strongholds to *fortify and protect and defend* what we have chosen to believe about ourselves, about others, about Satan, and about God.

12. Satan has no power over you unless you give him room, opportunities, and footholds in your life.

Chapter 3

Cooperating With Your New Creature Transformation

Transformation in Progress!

Second Corinthians 5:17 (NIV) says that if we are in Christ, we are a new creature. The old is gone and the new has come. This is great news for all of us who believe that we are in Him and He is in us. Still, we have to admit that few of us really walk consistently as that promised new creation. I certainly know that it isn't my new creature who keeps getting its feet tangled up and tripping all over itself—it's my old creature trying to walk for me!

> It's time to hold up a white flag of surrender, break down your self-defense systems, deep-six your soul's religiosity, and kick out its junkyard guard dogs!

So it makes sense that I need to figure out how to get the old creature—the old nature—in my soul transitioned into my new creature. How can any of us walk in the Spirit when our feet are mired down in our unsurrendered souls' junkyard?

Think for a moment about the ugly fuzzy caterpillar who is simply eating and waiting for a later new creature phase of its life. Who could possibly see the potential beauty yet to come out of that little hairy thing creeping along a branch? Yet that caterpillar is going to go through a metamorphosis phase that will transition it from ugly to gorgeous with big, gloriously colored silky wings that it can soar upon right up towards the sky.

The Greek word *metamorphoo* is translated in our Bibles as "transform" or "transformation" according to *Thayer's Greek/ English Lexicon of the New Testament.* The transformation of our old creatures (unsurrendered

Transformed means
to be changed into
another form.

souls) into our new creatures (souls fully surrendered to God) comes about in two different manners.

In 2 Corinthians 3:14-18 (NKJV) we read how those who believe in Jesus Christ will be changed by the Spirit of the Lord. The Jews' minds were blinded to their Messiah, and they refused to acknowledge Jesus Christ to be Him. This passage says that same blindness, the veil, is still unlifted in the Jewish hearts. Only when a Jew or Gentile recognizes Christ as Savior, the Messiah, is that blindness lifted so the Spirit of God can begin the work of transforming the believer into His image.

> *"But their minds were blinded. For until this day the same veil remains unlifted in the reading of the Old Testament, because the veil is taken away in Christ. But even to this day, when Moses is read, a veil lies on their heart. Nevertheless, when one turns to the Lord, the veil is taken away. Now the Lord is the Spirit; and where the Spirit of the Lord is, there is liberty. But we all, with unveiled face, beholding as in a mirror the glory of the Lord, are being transformed into the same image from glory to glory, just as by the Spirit of the Lord."*

The second manner of being transformed into His image comes through our cooperation with the work of the Spirit of God in the renewing of our minds. Romans 12:2 (AMP) tell us that through the renewing of our minds, we will be changed. We can cooperate with this renewal by studying the Word of God, by repenting of our sins, and by loosing our souls' industrial-strength Velcro grip on its wrong beliefs and bad attitudes:

> *"Do not be conformed to this world (this age), [fashioned after and adapted to its external, superficial customs], but be transformed (changed) by the [entire] renewal of your mind [by its new ideals and its new attitude], so that you may prove [for yourselves] what is the good and acceptable and perfect will of God, even the thing which is good and acceptable and perfect [in His sight for you]."*

We are in transition mode, brothers and sisters. We are being transformed from our original caterpillar/grub state to the beautiful freedom of our butterfly state. Cooperate with the transition—do all that you can to surrender to this miraculous transformation.

Cooperating With Transformation

God will eventually pressure your soul into being transformed into a surrendered butterfly status, but there is a faster way to break down its opposition. To hasten the process, part one of cooperating with your transformation begins with praying the binding prayers to stabilize and steady yourself and praying the loosing prayers to destroy your unsurrendered soul's strongholds and old ways. While your soul's strongholds are trying to hide your guilt and pain over your sins, they are

BEYOND Shattered Strongholds

also preserving the anxiety and fear that comes out of your unresolved issues. They have to go!

Proverbs 28:13 (AMP) tells you how to cooperate with the next part of the transformation process:

"He who covers his transgressions will not prosper, but whoever confesses and forsakes his sins will obtain mercy."

Acknowledging, confessing, and forsaking your sins is the second step of cooperating with the transformation process. This is much easier for you to do once you have begun clearing out your soul's old rubble. Sin can hide in a very small amount of rubble that might be left behind.

> Nehemiah's work is a type of the Holy Spirit's difficulty in renewing your soul because of all the rubble in it.

Nehemiah is considered to be a type of the Holy Spirit in the Old Testament, his name meaning "Jehovah consoles" or "comforted by God." In Nehemiah 4:10, we read that Nehemiah's restoration of the walls of the city of Jerusalem was being held up because of all of the rubble that was in the way of the builders. Whenever you are loosing wrong patterns of thinking, wrong ideas, and misconceptions from your soul, you are choosing to clear the rubble out of it to make room for the Holy Spirit's renewal work.

Part three of cooperating with the transformation process can be found in David's words in Psalms 32:5 (AMP):

*"I acknowledged my sin to You, and my iniquity I did not hide. I said, I will confess my transgressions to the Lord [**continually unfolding the past till all is***

told]—then You [instantly] forgave me the guilt and iniquity of my sin."

Some believe that the new birth spiritual transaction of accepting Christ as their Lord and Savior (in exchange for forgiveness and freedom from guilt) was a once-and-for-all deal that automatically took care of any sins they might commit in their futures as well. Many have used this belief to resist realizing that unforgiveness on their part can keep them from being forgiven. You have to be forgiven to get into heaven. You do the math.

The caveat (qualification or stipulation) to being forgiven on an ongoing basis is that you must repent of the sins you commit as a Christian, and you must forgive others of their sins against you whether they repent or not.

The need to repent of your sins did not end with your new birth. In the Book of Revelation, we can read Jesus' own words to the Church of Ephesus in Revelation 2:2-5 (NKJV):

> *"I know your works, your labor, your patience, and that you cannot bear those who are evil. And you have tested those who say they are apostles and are not, and have found them liars; and you have persevered and have patience, and have labored for My name's sake and have not become weary. Nevertheless I have this against you, that you have left your first love. Remember therefore from where you have fallen; repent and do the first works, or else I will come to you quickly and remove your lampstand from its place—**unless you repent.**"*

Repenting is still in style right through the Book of Revelation.

The Apostle Paul said in 2 Corinthians 7:9-10 (AMP):

> *"I am glad now, not because you were pained, but because you were pained into repentance [and so turned back to God]; for you felt a grief such as God meant you to feel, so that in nothing you might suffer loss through us or harm for what we did. For godly grief and the pain God is permitted to direct, produce a repentance that leads and contributes to salvation and deliverance from evil, and it never brings regret; but worldly grief (the hopeless sorrow that is characteristic of the pagan world) is deadly [breeding and ending in death]."*

Many, many layers of self-protection and corresponding beliefs have been established by your soul over the years of your life, and some perseverance will be required to uncover them all. Just know that you are working towards a very positive goal of complete surrender and freedom from your past. It is doable! Here is a simple binding and loosing prayer to get started:

Father, I thank you for the Keys of the Kingdom. I choose to bind my will, my mind, and my emotions to your plans for my life. I loose, smash, crush, and destroy the stronghold thinking, wrong beliefs, wrong ideas, and misconceptions of my soul which are like rubble getting in the way of my soul's restoration. I am sorry and I do repent for not having done this sooner. I will change and force my soul to give up and turn away from its old ways. Your Word says that to repent means to think differently, to change my mind, to regret my sins, and to change my conduct. I am choosing to do this. Thank

you, Jesus, for giving me these keys and the guidelines
of the Word to help me cooperate with my healing and
restoration. Amen.

Where's The Power?

In my early years as a Christian, I did not understand why
the Word of God wasn't manifesting itself in power in my life
with signs and wonders following—just like the Bible said it
should. I memorized the power verses and quoted them—I
even yelled them at the devil—but nothing ever seemed to
change.

I felt completely defeated when I gave up on getting the victory
and just slipped back into old patterns. Knowing others with
the same problem, I wondered if we really were all destined
to become new creatures like it says in 2 Corinthians 5:17.

In the original *Shattering Your Strongholds*, I wrote of a
woman named Trudy who had accepted Jesus as her Savior, but
that was the only connection to heaven she wanted. Having
experienced a traumatic relationship with her earthly father
who was a violent alcoholic, Trudy associated fear and pain
with any entity named "father." She certainly did not trust an
all-powerful heavenly Father's motives.

Trudy only saw God through the emotional baggage of her
childhood spent with a father figure she had learned to distrust.
She went to church, tithed, read the Bible, and prayed to Jesus.
But she had no intention of giving any more of herself than
that to any divine relationship.

Every time Trudy heard anything from the pulpit that named
God as the Father of all believers, she would experience
emotional whiplash. To Trudy, the word "father" meant

pain, rejection, humiliation, being unlovable, and feeling worthless. To other Christians, the word "Father" meant love, mercy, grace, and truth. Trudy knew nothing of love, mercy, grace, truth, or trust, and it seemed that no amount of teaching from the pulpit would ever penetrate her mind set about "fathers."

Her unresolved pain (rubble) so twisted the truth of God that it could not overcome the stronghold walls of her heart. Even I wondered if God's truth only worked for some people.

The mystery factors between who receives God's love and tender care and who doesn't are the height, the depth, and the thickness of their strongholds. These are factors that only God is fully aware of. Big strongholds that have been in place for a long time will filter out a lot of the truth that tries to work its way into someone's innermost being.

Consider what happens when you take crystal-clear water and pour it into a dirty filtering system. The clean water comes out the other side of the filter polluted and cloudy. The end result has nothing to do with the clean water poured in—but it has everything to do with the height, the depth, and the thickness of the dirt and debris in the filter it is poured through.

Filters on Overload

A mind filled with rubble from the past is a mind that will cloud any truth it receives today. Emotions filled with frightening memories, unexpressed anger, and fear will react against any incoming truths that that are not recognized as safe and acceptable. The will that is always on red

> Our souls function as filters for everything we have ever heard and experienced.

alert and ready to react to whatever frightens the mind or scorches the emotions is never more than one reaction away from initiating its fight or flight syndrome.

When the unsurrendered soul is in that condition, it is simply unable to receive help from God. God keeps speaking into the born-again spirit, which keeps trying to pass His words on into the soul, but this process must be completed like the passing of the baton in a relay race. If you have a runner who doesn't want to take the baton, the race is going to be lost. First Corinthians 2:14 (TM) tells us this:

> *"The unspiritual self (the unsurrendered soul), just as it is by nature, can't receive the gifts of God's Spirit. There's no capacity for them. They seem like so much silliness. Spirit can be known only by spirit—God's Spirit and our spirits in open communion."*

Strongholds in your soul will always prevent God's incoming "messages" from arriving intact. Your mind's whole focus will be upon whether or not these messages will upset the soul's balance. Your emotions will usually throw up reactions that only complicate your understanding. Based upon this input, your will usually reacts in a defensive mode. If the consensus of the soul is to reject what God has said, the will then commands the body to stand down—to take no action.

Christians have been taught that many of their problems and mistakes have happened because the devil has hijacked the control of their lives. The comedian Flip Wilson used to say, "The devil made me do it." Unfortunately some Christians don't know that Flip Wilson was just telling another one of his jokes. The real issue that nobody seems to get is that the devil can't force us to do anything we don't already have a leaning towards doing in the first place.

This prayer can help you begin to open up your spirit-to-soul lines of communication so that God's Word starts getting through the system of your unsurrendered soul:

> **I will open up my lines of communication to you, Father. I bind my will and my mind to your will, and I loose all deception, wrong patterns of thinking, and stronghold thinking from my soul. Call my attention to the blockades in my soul, and I will pull them down. Help me move all of the fear and reactions out of my soul whenever you speak. Help me to know where my soul has established its own lines of communication and rejected yours. Show me where the strongholds still stand, and I will pull them down. I want to hear your voice and obey your words. I believe you will help me to learn how to do this. Amen.**

You can eventually learn to accept God's words by sheer determination to have what He wants to give to you. People have been breaking through their own rubble and receiving God's healing power for centuries. The Apostle Paul was still struggling to do this even long after he had been born again and called to be a witness of Jesus Christ. The only problem by doing it with sheer will power and grit is that it takes so very long and it can wear you out!

The Apostle Paul's Transparency

We can all thank God for Paul's willingness to be so transparent in his letter to the Roman Christians, written years after he had been preaching the Good News (some sources say he wrote the Epistle to the Romans sometime around A.D. 56, nearly 20 years after he accepted Christ as his Lord and Master). In Romans 7:15-23 (TM), as Paul is expounding about the

Law, we read his confessions of trying to deal with his own unsurrendered soul:

> *"What I don't understand about myself is that I decide one way, but then I act another, doing things I absolutely despise … I realize that I don't have what it takes. I can will it, but I can't do it. I decide to do good, but I don't really do it; I decide not to do bad, but then I do it anyway. My decisions, such as they are, don't result in actions. Something has gone wrong deep within me and gets the better of me every time. It happens so regularly that it's predictable. The moment I decide to do good, sin is there to trip me up. I truly delight in God's commands, but it's pretty obvious that not all of me joins in that delight. Parts of me covertly rebel, and just when I least expect it, they take charge."*

Paul then admitted that he realized he didn't have what it took to do right but he knew who did. Romans 7:24-25 (TM) tells us this:

> *"I've tried everything and nothing helps. I'm at the end of my rope. Is there no one who can do anything for me? Isn't that the real question? The answer, thank God, is that Jesus Christ can and does. He acted to set things right in this life of contradictions where I want to serve God with all my heart and mind, but am pulled by the influence of sin to do something totally different."*

Our answer is in Jesus, as well. Jesus Christ has made a way for us to overcome all of the contradictions of life that we have ever experienced and all of the wrong things that we have done—everything! He died and shed His blood to give us a fresh start, to give us hope for a shiny new future. He is sitting in heaven at the right hand of the Father right now ever making intercession for us. He's given us the Keys of the Kingdom down here to get rid of our human baggage to make room to receive all He's asking the Father to give us.

Turn back to Trudy for a moment. The pain and needs that still existed in Trudy's soul even after she became a Christian allowed the enemy to continue deceiving and pushing her into building ever higher walls of distrust and fear. Those reinforced walls kept out all input from God because she had programmed herself to receive only what reinforced those things she already believed. This allowed Satan to replay her past to mess up her present to destroy her hope for a future.

Trudy's pain continued far too long after she became a Christian. She didn't realize that Jesus had answers for her to help her to understand her heavenly Father's love. God will use time to cause our faith to grow, but all too often, time lost in our lives has no mysterious spiritual meaning at all! Unredeemed time continues to tick away while God has to deal with our stubborn wills to get us to let go, strip off, and give up the toxic waste in our souls.

How wasteful is that?

On Top of Old Shattered Strongholds

The ultimate goal of the Keys of the Kingdom prayer principles is to surrender your soul, surrender to God's will, and then begin producing lots of fruit for the Kingdom of God. That news flash will NOT appeal to your unsurrendered soul, but will cause it to try to dig up some of its dirtiest old tricks. You need to constantly wash and rewash your unsurrendered soul just like a cat who just had a run-in with a skunk. Then read the Word to it while forcing it to pray prayers that obligate itself to God.

For some reason, that word picture amuses me no end. I can picture in full color my unsurrendered soul looking like some fuzzed up, sudsy, wet cat HATING the bath I'm giving it, but unable to get away. Not only that, but I'm reading Scripture to it and making it hold its paws in a praying position. Now that's priceless!

Regardless of whatever picture your unsurrendered soul conjures up, God cannot allow you to hang onto its baggage. You are never going to influence the people of this generation if you are always dragging stronghold baggage around with you.

You always have a choice—either choose to get rid of your wrong patterns of thinking or choose to cling to them. You might think you don't have any wrong patterns of thinking. It is still a good thing to bind your mind to the mind of Christ and loose wrong patterns of thinking. If you do have them, they will have to go after some focused loosing on your part. If you don't have them, it will be like taking a bath when you aren't dirty. You won't hurt a thing, but you might smell a little sweeter.

Being clean brings up many good options. The Word of God says that Eliphaz told Job that if his hands were clean (if his life was right with God), his prayers could deliver sinners. The prayer of one who is in right standing has truly awesome power to impact lives because God *"will even deliver the one (for whom you intercede) who is not innocent; yes, he will be delivered through the cleanness of your hands"* (Job 22:30, AMP).

No one but God knows can tell how many loved ones have been spared, even saved, because of the intercessions of a righteous person. When you have loosed all that you know how to loose from your soul's record-keeping system as you pray, your prayers can begin to save some from ruin.

Reconciliation, Restoration, Renovation, and Refreshing!

The Word says God has committed unto us the ministry and the word of reconciliation (2 Corinthians 5:18-19). The Greek word for "reconciliation" in these verses is *katallage*, which mean to exchange or restore to favor with God. Part of this occurs as we are transformed by the renewing (renovation) of our minds (Romans 12:2). Webster's Dictionary says that "renew" means to restore, rebuild, reestablish, and renovate. Don't you just hate the "UN" words (unloved, unworthy, etc.) and love the "RE" words?

Acts 3:19 (Amplified) records these words:

> "*So repent (change your mind and purpose); turn around and return (to God), that your sins may be erased (blotted out, wiped clean),* **that times of refreshing—of recovering from the effects of heat, of reviving with fresh air—may come from the presence of the Lord.**"

We can be refreshed and revived, and recover from the effects of previous experiences—wow! This is truly the blessing of being a child of God. How much easier it will be to receive all this if we use the keys of binding and loosing to clear plenty of room to receive it. God has promised restoration all through His Word.

"Behold, I will send you Elijah the prophet before the great and terrible day of the Lord comes. And he shall turn (and reconcile) the hearts of the (estranged) fathers to the (ungodly) children, and the hearts of the (rebellious) children to (the piety of) their fathers (a reconciliation produced by repentance of the ungodly ...)" Malachi 4:5-6 (AMP). RESTORATION.

"After those days, saith the Lord, I will put my law in their inward parts, and write it in their hearts; and will be their God, and they shall be my people" Jeremiah 31:33 (KJV). RESTORATION.

"And I will restore to you the years that the locust hath eaten, the cankerworm, and the caterpillar, and the palmerworm, my great army which I sent among you. And ye shall eat in plenty, and be satisfied, and praise the name of the Lord your God, that hath dealt wondrously with you: and my people shall never be ashamed" Joel 2:25-26 (KJV). RESTORATION.

"But be transformed (changed) by the (entire) renewal of your mind—by its new ideals and its new attitude—so that you may prove (for yourselves) what is the good and acceptable and perfect will of God" Romans 12:2 (AMP). RESTORATION.

God has always wanted to restore men and women to Himself. He sent His Son to die on the cross to bring about a blood-bought way for man to come fully into that restoration. Jesus is now being retained in heaven until this has been fully accomplished. We can cooperate with this restoration by making room to receive it.

How to Receive This R&R

Romans 8:4 (TM) reminds us that we do not change ourselves by trying to follow the Bible's rules and regulations. We do not become better people by trying harder. We just need to cooperate with whatever God's Spirit is wanting to do:

> *"And now what the law code asked for but we couldn't deliver is accomplished as we, instead of redoubling our own efforts, simply embrace what the Spirit is doing in us."*

Romans 10:9-10 (TM) tells us that we just need to:

> *"Say the welcoming word to God—'Jesus is my Master'—embracing, body and soul, God's work of doing in us what he did in raising Jesus from the dead. That's it. You're not 'doing' anything; you're simply calling out to God, trusting him to do it for you. That's salvation. With your whole being you embrace God setting things right, and then you say it, right out loud: 'God has set everything right between him and me!'"*

God has made everything right between you and Him from His end, and you just need to receive that as truth on your end. It can be difficult to receive a miracle truth when you have refuse and rubble in your soul. That is why it is another miracle that Jesus has left you the Keys of the Kingdom. These keys are able to start getting rid of your soul's residue left from everything that ever been said to you, done to you, or taken from you.

How do we find time to spend hours praying to open up paths in the spirit world so that we can go out into the world and lead captives free or go into the hospitals and heal the sick? Life today is filled with stress and pressure, struggles, and unpaid bills. Indeed, who has time for such things? Such pressures do not sound like the

> It is a victory to turn a hard time into a growth experience, rather than letting it cause you to feel like you cannot go forward.

molding experience required for overcoming Christians, but they can be if you cooperate with what God wants to do in you through them.

In 2003, I lost both of my parents. I have no brothers and sisters, so it was a lonely experience. I spent nearly nine months of 2003 traveling 400 miles round trip every week to make sure my parents were being taken care of in a skilled nursing home and that their bills were paid, the cats were fed, the lawns were watered, and their laundry was done. Then I went back home and spent two days in my ministry office taking care of business, finally trying to put myself back together over the weekend before the next week started all over again.

My mother had many health problems that required skilled care around the clock. After an exhausting month of scheduling caregivers and being a caregiver myself, I realized that my mother's health was deteriorating quickly. She had congestive heart failure, diabetes, high blood pressure, and early dementia. Then my father passed away in May. My mom could not grasp that he was gone, and I was always trying to explain to her that he neither in another wing of the hospital nor waiting for her at home.

I remember speaking to my spiritual mentor, Iverna Tompkins, about what was the right thing for me to do. As a daughter and an only child, should I shut down my ministry and move 200 miles away to try to care full-time for my mother? My mentor said that all she got when she prayed was that I should keep doing exactly what I was doing until the Lord told me differently. She assured me that He would see me through any decisions I had to make.

I prayed the binding and loosing prayers more than I ever had before. They helped me stay connected to God who was in my life when everything else going on around me seemed like sinking sand.

In October, while staying at my parents' home, I came down with acute pancreatitis. I had to be airlifted back to Sacramento for surgery. Three weeks later when I had recovered enough to drive back up to visit my mother again, the telephone rang as I was packing the car for the trip. My mother had just died—alone in the skilled nursing home with no family members with her.

My parents were both dead within six months of each other; my ministry was surviving but definitely not thriving; my new book and correspondence course deadlines were in shambles; I felt terrible guilt over not being with my mom when she died; and I was fast developing terrible pains of arthritis in my right hip. Okay, we're tribulating here.

I managed to move on through the early part of 2004 on autopilot until I finally had to have hip surgery the first week of September. I had a three-week speaking tour through the Midwest and on to the East Coast pending in just six weeks.

Important Point Here: Many people fear what the binding and loosing prayers will kick loose in their souls. This is because they do not realize the greater danger of what their souls have buried inside of them. Every ugly and fearful thing that is buried in your soul is leaking toxic waste (mental, emotional, and chemical) into your body—your whole being—every day. Things might look all right on the surface, but decay and destruction to your immune system,

> Keys of the Kingdom prayers help you to bring toxic things in your soul to the surface so that God can fix what is broken so you can get well and be whole.

your brain cells, your internal organs, and your nervous system is going on just below the surface of your consciousness.

Ah, but life still keeps coming at you whether you are praying the binding and loosing prayers or not. These prayers won't hide you from the storm; they will help you walk through the storm with your head held high. It might be better to be wearing the raincoat, but the raincoat won't stop the storm.

Let me bring the important point home here: Everything that happened in my life in 2003 and 2004 *was a result of life's inevitable circumstances. The things that I went through were not caused by the binding and loosing prayers.* The deaths of my parents, my surgeries, and the other things that happened were already invisibly scheduled on my day planner since the day I was born. I just didn't know it when I ordered my day planners. The binding and loosing prayers, however, held me incredibly steady and snugged up to Jesus when I felt I just couldn't get through the fog anymore.

After the hip replacement surgery, I remember thinking (while in a haze of pain pills) that my ministry as well as my purpose in life was probably over. I had only had 63 years of good use in me for the Lord, and now they were all used up. The Vicodin and the Valium

> I felt that my life was winding down; it was time to just sit on the porch, hum some hymns, and think about the good old days.

were creating a soft little buzz: "Oh, well, what's the use of trying anymore? Let's just goooo with the flow."

I was so medicated, I hadn't been praying or reading the Word for several days, but the binding and loosing prayers of others were sustaining me. The previous workings of the binding and loosing prayers I had prayed were sustaining me as well. About six days after my surgery, the Lord clearly spoke to me and told me to look up 2 Corinthians 4:16 in The Message and to personalize it and make it mine! I did and I was overwhelmed by what I read:

> "So (I'm) not giving up. How could (I)! Even though on the outside it often looks like things are falling apart on (me), on the inside, where God is making new life, not a day goes by without his unfolding grace."

I actually had devotionals for the next two days on just this one Scripture! The Word of God can be so very personal and specific when you need it. And I needed it—I needed it bad. I began to cling to the words that said His grace was unfolding in my life every day.

I said those words over and over to try to hold back my feelings of guilt about all the missed deadlines over the past year and all of the back work piled up at the office, plus having to finish handling all of my parents' affairs. Then the Lord spoke to me again and said to look up 2 Corinthians 8:10-12 in The Message and to personalize the verses and make their words mine. I eagerly grabbed my Bible and began to read:

> "So here's what I think: The best thing you can do right now is to finish what you started last year and not let those good intentions grow stale. Your heart's been in the right place all along. You've got what it takes to

finish it up, so go to it. Once the commitment is clear, you do what you can, not what you can't. The heart regulates the hands."

These verses were like a spring of restoration to my soul. I felt the guilt lift and I felt encouragement to get up and get on with my life. Just over five weeks later, I flew to Indiana for previously scheduled meetings and a television appearance, then on to New Jersey and Florida for meetings and television appearances. One week later, I flew back across the nation to New Jersey for more meetings. While I may not have been moving at the speed of light, life began to feel good again, and I was setting my feet on whatever path the Lord provided.

Did the enemy try to create additional pain and trouble during this difficult time? Sure he did! But hell is only able to sustain its program against you when it is not resisted. When your soul is unsurrendered and wanting to pursue its own agendas, it is in opposition to the leadings of your born-again spirit. You are like a house divided. A house divided is a house that opposes itself and opens the door to the enemy's mischief.

Personal Programs Do Not Bring Renewal

The Bible gives no record of Saul of Tarsus having to find a counselor or a support group to overcome the guilt of his treacherous past—nor did Peter for his monumental failings—nor did Moses for his anger and act of murder—nor did David for arranging the murder of Bathsheba's husband.

> Jesus told the woman caught in adultery that she was not condemned by Him, and no one else had the courage to condemn her in His presence. These words brought her full spiritual and emotional freedom.

Jesus did not send the woman caught in adultery (in John 8:11) away to seek therapy or to undergo rehabilitation. He simply told her that there was not one left to condemn her and He did not either. Then He said, *"Go and sin no more."*

Beautiful words from the living Word, Jesus Christ. Note that He forgave her of her past and her guilt, and He directed her towards her future. Every one of these biblical figures received mercy and grace (healing) from the Lord.

You simply cannot heal yourself by a strong will to survive or by working a "program." You are healed by surrendering everything in your life—past, present and future—to the will of God and then *receiving healing from Him.* This can be a fearful thing if you have always managed to avoid dealing directly with God. But there has to come a time when you finally want to be free so bad, you're willing to face your fears.

If a counselor, program, or group has helped you come to this point, then they have served you well. But they cannot heal you or set you truly free. You cannot set yourself free—but you can begin the process of surrendering your way to complete freedom in His will. You can tear down your strongholds to make room in your soul for God to fill you with power, strength, and words of peace and love for your generation. Romans 8:5-6, (TM), tells us this:

> *"Those who think they can do it on their own end up obsessed with measuring their own moral muscle but never get around to exercising it in real life. Those who trust God's action in them find that God's Spirit is in them—living and breathing God! Obsession with self in these matters is a dead end; attention to God leads us out into the open, into a spacious, free life."*

A New Word About Strongholds

In the original *Shattering Your Strongholds*, I wrote that strongholds could be named: i.e. stronghold of fear, stronghold of doubt, stronghold of anger, etc. The problem with writing a book at any time is that there are always new pieces that come into your understanding as you teach and walk out the revelation you have written about.

Strongholds are actually the framework of how your soul goes about rationalizing and justifying holding onto its wrong beliefs, wrong ideas, wrong patterns of thinking, denial, and deception. They are a framework that protects something you need to get rid of.

Your strongholds may have actually enabled you to survive terrifying circumstances in your past that you had no control over. The fact that they seemed to protect you then is one of the reasons you still trust them today. But if that same stronghold thinking is still in place in your life, it is providing access for the enemy's assaults today. It is also protecting wrong beliefs that you have learned to believe in more than you believe in what God has said. That is sin.

Strongholds are what you rely upon to defend and protect your right to believe something or to protect something that your soul greatly fears will be exposed. For example, being painfully deceived by people that you trusted can cause your soul to justify believing that you must protect yourself against ever being deceived again. Defending this wrong belief will even cause you to resist intimacy with God. This is not a stronghold of defense; this is a stronghold built to protect your right to be defensive.

If you have serious doubts about whether or not the Word of God will work for you, your soul may build a stronghold to protect your right to resist "falling for" the promises in the Word. This attitude can turn into cynicism over anything God's Word says. This is not a stronghold of doubt; it is a stronghold built to defend your right to doubt God's Word.

Being rejected can cause your wounded soul to build stronghold walls to protect a false belief that you cannot be rejected anymore. This stronghold also protects the façade that you might try to project of being independent and completely self-sufficient with no need for relationship with anyone. Strongholds can fortify and protect your right to avoid being vulnerable to anyone. This will often transition into your soul's fear of even being vulnerable to the work of the Holy Spirit. This is not a stronghold of rejection; it is a stronghold built to protect your wrong beliefs about what you have to do be prevent being rejected again.

If you have a lot of unmet needs, your soul may hide them behind a stronghold it builds to defend your false belief that you are totally secure without any needs of any kind. This false belief can help you project a façade of strength intended to keep others from knowing how internally fragile and needy you really are. This can extend to keeping God at arm's length, as well. This is not a stronghold of neediness; it is a stronghold protecting a false belief and façade of having no need of anything or anyone.

If you feel that you can never forgive someone for what they have done to you, your soul may build a stronghold to rationalize defending your hard feeling, bitterness, and anger towards that person. A stronghold can also protect your belief in the lie that God doesn't expect you to forgive because what happened to you is just too unforgivable. This same stronghold may also justify your adopting a victim mentality. This is not a stronghold of unforgiveness; it is a stronghold built to protect denial and deception regarding God's command that you must forgive.

Betrayal can cause a wounded soul to build a stronghold to protect your right to prevent anyone from ever getting too close to you again. When you build strongholds to protect your emotional wounds from betrayal, you generally will have a hard time fully trusting God, too. His perfect love casts out fear, but you remain in your fear in order to feel safe. This is not a stronghold of betrayal; it is a stronghold built to protect yourself against intimacy.

If you had a childhood filled with chaos, instability, and everything seemingly out of control, your soul may have built a stronghold to protect your right to defend yourself against being at the mercy of others. Your soul may also build a network of strongholds to defend your right to build boundaries and rules and regulations to deal with the people around you. This is not a stronghold of control; it is a stronghold built to justify setting rigid boundaries and regulations against people your soul believes will take advantage of you.

If you always felt deprived and unappreciated, your soul most likely will have built strongholds to justify and protect your right to indulge yourself inappropriately to compensate for your unmet needs and pain. This wrong belief also justifies the right to chemically alter any sense of reality with drugs or alcohol to blot out pain. This is not a stronghold of indulgence; it is a complex set up of rationalizations for why you should do whatever you want to in order to compensate for your own pain.

If you have grown up with a great deal of fear, your soul may build strongholds around apprehensive and anxious feelings over unresolved issues is your life. These strongholds help you rationalize and justify your fears as being normal and acceptable. You can avoid dealing with the fear as long as your soul runs the lie on you that you are fine. This is not a stronghold of fear; it is a stronghold designed to avoid all things that can trigger your fear reactions.

Denial refuses to acknowledge any of the above things. Denial is a valid, temporary, mental and emotional coping mechanism to enable the human mind to survive certain traumatic situations—similar to how shock prevents a severely wounded body from immediate death. Denial can enable abused children to survive unbearable situations. But just as shock becomes dangerous and life-threatening when a person cannot come out of it, so does denial. Denial can kill you when you refuse to acknowledge health issues, foolish choices, even dangerous relationships. This is not a stronghold of denial; it is a stronghold that helps you to rationalize denying whatever you want.

These are some of the reasons our souls build strongholds around things we cannot bear to face. You can loose the grip of every one of them and what they are protecting in your life, thereby making room to receive that which is right and healing. The binding and loosing keys that accomplish this are ours by the grace of God and the power of the resurrected Lord Jesus Christ.

God generally will not forcibly take what you don't want to surrender. The excuse, "If God wants me to give it up, He'll take it from me," is old-nature, whitewashed, hogwashed nonsense! Stop believing that—it's not true. What you erroneously believe about yourself can be more powerful in shaping your life than any of God's truths. Praying this prayer can help you start sorting out your wrong beliefs, even your denial that they exist.

> Lord, I know that I need to do some soulish demolition and clean up. Just like urban renewal projects, I want to bring in the spiritual heavy equipment and bring down high walls that protecting deception and denial in me. My safety equipment is my ability to bind myself to you—body, soul, and spirit, which I now choose to do. My demolition equipment is to loose, smash, crush, and destroy all of my soul's wrong beliefs, its denial, and the deception and error that it keeps clinging to. I loose all these things right now, because I do not want any error standing between me and you. Thank you for these keys, Jesus. Amen.

Summary

1. Romans 12:2 (AMP) tells us that through the renewing of our minds, we will be changed.
2. A mind filled with rubble from the past is a mind that will cloud any truth it receives today.
3. Jesus Christ has made a way for us to overcome all of the contradictions of life that we have ever experienced and all of the wrong things that we have done—everything!
4. The ultimate goal of the Keys of the Kingdom prayer principles is to make your soul surrender to the will of God so that you can begin to produce fruit for the Kingdom of God.
5. You are never going to influence the people of this generation if you are always dragging stronghold baggage around with you.

6. You always have a choice—either choose to get rid of your wrong patterns of thinking or choose to cling to them.
7. God has made everything right between you and Him from His end—you just need to receive that as truth on your end.
8. Every ugly and fearful thing that is buried in your soul is leaking toxic waste into your body—into your whole being—every day.
9. Hell is only able to sustain its program against you when it is not resisted.
10. You are healed by surrendering everything in your life—past, present and future—to the will of God and then *receiving healing from Him.*
11. You cannot set yourself free. But you can begin surrendering your way to full freedom in Him.
12. What you erroneously believe about yourself can be more powerful in shaping your life than any of God's truths.

Chapter 4

Kingdom Key of Binding

Binding

I was very excited in 1986 to begin learning that there were far deeper meanings to the words "bind" and "binding"— meanings I had never heard before. To use the kingdom key of binding means to undergird, heal, hold, persuade, and steady yourself. It also means to cause fragmented pieces to come back into one whole, put oneself under obligation to, and to cling to (original Hebrew and Greek meanings).

In my previous fourteen years as a Christian, I had only been taught to use the key of binding to bind the devil. That seemed like a strange thing to do since it was obvious that the devil seemed to be stepping up his assaults on mankind, rather than slowing them down because everyone was "binding" him.

Research tools such as original language lexicons (the lexicons used in this message are *Gesenius' Hebrew/Chaldean Lexicon of the Old Testament* and *Thayer's Greek/English Lexicon of the New Testament*) show us how the word "bind" was used during the time of and in the context of each Scripture involved. Today's use of the word "bind" generally means to restrict, shackle, or *to tie up*. The use of the word "bind" in Matthew 16:19, 18:18 has a positive meaning: *to tie to*.

Other meanings of the word "bind" in the original Greek language of the New Testament are to weave together, wind around, cause many pieces to coalesce, and to obligate oneself to (someone).

Jesus said in Matthew 16:19 that whatever I bound on earth, it would be bound in heaven as well (if it was in accordance with the work He had left for me to do). I later realized that whatever Jesus had left for me to do was itself already bound to and part of the Father's will in heaven. These prayers allowed me to tie myself to the Father's will so that I might draw upon all of His power, resources, and love to complete what Jesus left for me to do.

> The binding prayers do not mean that God has to agree with whatever I pray.

The Keys of the Kingdom prayers allow me to be the point of agreement on earth with whatever God has determined is His will to accomplish. When I pray right prayers, agreeing that His will in heaven needs to be manifested in lives and circumstances on earth, God sees that it is done. Praying this way brings what God wants into being. However, the Keys of the Kingdom prayer principles will not get you what *you think you need* unless it is the same thing the *Father knows you need* to walk out your destiny purposes.

> Binding prayers are powerful, extremely effective, and can be very comforting.

These prayer keys allow you to come into agreement with God regarding your life and the lives of others to bring about a manifestation of His will. Some unsurrendered souls do not believe this is a good thing, but I find it a great comfort to know that I don't have to ferret out and analyze all of the details of a situation to pray effectively for everyone involved. When you pray for others to cause things in their lives to agree with what the Father has already established in heaven, the Father always does what is best for everyone.

It is a strange thing to my mind, but the Sovereign God over everything that exists in any realm has chosen to involve us in the playing out of His will here on earth. He looks for someone to agree with Him that He knows what is best in a given life or circumstance. I wonder if He doesn't sometimes walk up and down the edge of heaven saying, "Why won't someone agree that I can heal that man's cancer? Why won't someone agree with me that I can mend that marriage? Why won't someone agree that I not only know what is best, but I know exactly how to bring it to pass in those lives?"

Praying Right Prayers

Many people have been taught that prayers are what you say to God to get what you want—without having to worry about whether or not God agrees. This is one of the main reasons that many people get discouraged and disappointed in their prayer lives. When they pray amiss, the answers don't come! God has instituted prayer to build a relationship with

> I'm glad He did not give me all of the things I begged and pleaded for in prayer. Thank you, Lord, that for the most part you don't answer soulish prayers. Thank you, thank you!

you and to give you that point of agreement with Him. He doesn't want to answer prayers prayed amiss that will lead you into temptation or sorrow. He wants to have communion with you.

I have known God to answer some soulish prayers to accomplish His purposes in showing someone that what they thought they just had to have was not at all what was best for them. I can personally attest to that because in times past I learned the hard way that I was praying for things that had nothing to do with God's will for my life.

He finally gave me a couple of the wrong things I so badgered Him for. Guess what? I had a terrible time getting rid of them and their consequences! After a few go rounds like that, I began to agree with God that He knew more about what I needed in my life than I did. This is a hard thing to convince people of who have a lot of unmet needs in their lives.

I receive many e-mails from women and men who are very unhappy with their single lives, feeling that they have always been hurt in all of their relationships and God could send a mate to fix all that—if He wanted to. So, why wasn't He doing it, they wanted to know. They were actually scolding God for not answering their prayers.

In trying to answer them with wisdom and compassion, I stirred up hornet nests in two of them. I replied to their e-mails in this manner, telling them to bind themselves to God's will, their minds to the mind of Christ, and their emotions to the healing balance of the Holy Spirit:

> God has been protecting you from being so hurt again. Here is what I feel He wants for you: 1) He either wants you to want Him so much, you won't care if you get married or, 2) He wants you to want Him so much, you will trust Him to heal you so that you can have a balanced, whole relationship with a mate. Either way is a win-win situation, right? Loose your soul's desires for a mate for right now, and ask God to fix the brokenness in your soul/heart first. Loose all your feelings of anger, fear of getting older, and

being alone. You are so determined that only a relationship can fix your pain and need, I'm concerned. If you don't strip your soul of these patterns of thinking, they can drive you deeper into despair over being alone, perhaps even driving you into a wrong relationship. You need to let God make you whole to be a blessing to, and to be blessed by, a mate. If you will work with God and trust Him to heal your soul, then if you still want a mate, I believe God will bring you a major super spouse!

After I answered them, the scolding quickly turned from God towards me. Both writers said that I had taken away their hope of ever getting married—that I was trying to convince them they would never have someone in their lives. One was extremely angry with me. Their unsurrendered souls caused them to read what wasn't even there. I have prayed that these people would not continue to pray more urgent, desperate wrong prayers that would get no answers, making them feel even more alienated from God.

One person wrote me about my saying that it was not wise to pray for a specific person to be your mate, rather to bind yourself to God's will while losing wrong patterns of thinking and stronghold thinking. I reminded this person that our heavenly Father knew exactly who He had chosen as a perfect mate and that this person would never be sorry for waiting. Then I asked this person to pray this:

> **Lord, please help me relax in your timing and your plans for my life. I bind myself, body, soul, and spirit, to your will. I want to be whole, so please help me understand how to cooperate with your healing work in every area of my soul. I loose all of my soul's wrong beliefs and attitudes that you don't care if I'm happy or not. I know that you do care, but I am going to believe that you alone know what is best for me and what will make me**

the happiest. I love you, Lord, and I long to know you better. Amen.

Cutting Through the Clutter

Binding and loosing prayers allow you to get to the heart of a situation in your life or in someone else's life without wading through all the gory details, without soulish judgments, and without blind choices being made. Unfortunately, not everyone agrees that this is good. I've been dropped from more than one prayer chain because I didn't want to listen to the personal details of prayer requests, nor would I agree to pass the details on to the next person on the chain "so they would know what to pray."

> Arghhhhhh! I feel just like Charlie Brown every time I hear someone say that.

We get many prayer requests coming into our office by telephone, as well as by snail mail and e-mail. I always ask my staff to not allow the person to give more than a couple of minutes worth of explanation, letting the caller do that only so he or she would feel more secure that we knew what to pray. There is no situation that requires more than a few minutes of explanation before you pray. More explanation than that and the poor caller would only be reinforcing their doubts and concerns.

One lady called our office and I happened to pick up the line. She asked me to pray for her son and daughter-in-law who were having to drive the full length of Florida, and a hurricane warning had just been issued for the area they would be driving through. I prayed and bound everyone in the path of that hurricane to God's will and purposes, and I loosed the works of the enemy from all of them. Then I asked for God's mercy, grace, and protection for every person who was in the hurricane's path and said amen.

After about a fifteen-second pause, she said, "But you didn't pray for my son and daughter-in-law." I replied that I really had. She said, "No, you didn't. I need to have specific prayers prayed."

I said, "But God doesn't. He wants someone to agree with Him that His protection and mercy will be with whoever is in the way of great danger right now." These prayers seek for God's will and Christ's thoughts and the Holy Spirit's healing comfort in each situation you apply them to. Whenever you pray with these keys in this manner, you are establishing the agreement link with God's will in heaven and leaving the details to Him!

Binding prayers do this—they:

1. Stabilize you in your thinking
2. Steady you in your walk
3. Give you a spiritual safety harness attached to His will
4. Give you a spiritual seat belt for when He calls you to come up higher

In the original *Shattering Your Strongholds*, I explained the key of binding by using the example of parents binding babies to their bodies with cloth baby wraps used in the sixties and seventies in the United States, as well as in many other countries. When the baby was bound to the parent, wherever the parent went, the baby went. The baby had its own personality and thoughts, but it was bound to and experiencing the more mature will and choices of the parent.

This seemed like an exciting word picture of being bound to the will of God.

I learned through experience that binding myself to His will was always a steady, stabilizing thing to do when I was in any kind of difficult circumstance.

I also learned that I was not going to get what my soul desired from binding myself to things that were not in God's will. I have to admit that I really was hoping that this might work at least sometimes. I could think of all kinds of things that I would have liked to bind myself to: Tom Selleck, a candy-apple red Lamborghini, the lottery, and so forth. But God obviously did not think I need any of these "things" to finish the work Jesus left for me to do.

Whenever I tried praying these self-agenda types of binding prayers in the early stages of my understanding of the keys—even when I prayed them in the name of Jesus—it was a lost cause.

Binding In His Name

Many have wondered (as I also used to) why John 14:13-14 seemed to tell us that whatever we asked in Jesus' name, He would do. We've all asked Him to do things based upon this "promise," and then He seemed to do nothing. The Message translates these verses this way:

> "From now on, whatever you request along the lines of who I am and what I am doing, I'll do it. That's how the Father will be seen for who he is in the Son. I mean it. Whatever you request in this way, I'll do."

Matthew Henry's Commentary on the Whole Bible tells us that Jesus was saying this in John 14:12-14:

"Ask any thing that is good and proper . . . assistance in your work, for a mouth and wisdom, for preservation out of the hands of your enemies, for power to work miracles when there is occasion, for the success of the ministry in the conversion of souls; ask to be informed, directed, indicated."

John 14:13 must be seen as the continuation of verse 12 where Jesus has just said that we would do greater works than He had done. In order for us to do these things for

> He never asks us to do anything that He does not provide the resources for us to finish the work.

the Kingdom of God, He was making himself available to see that we would have whatever we needed to finish the work He was assigning to us. Christians have taken verse 13 completely out of context, believing that it promises a blank check to request anything we want, even if we would consume it upon our own lusts.

This explains why all of us have at one time or another prayed in Jesus' name (asking for something that was not necessary for our completion of the work He has left for us to do), and we did not get answers from the Father.

While my soul was not completely happy about this piece of information, I felt a new steadiness in my thoughts and my words. I felt I was lining up with God's will more than I ever had before. I actually felt as if I had a spiritual safety harness and a spiritual seat belt.

I have always been excited about binding myself to the truth of God. Deception often comes in degrees of off white and pale grey that can be misinterpreted by the human senses and the human mind. Binding myself to the truth of God helped me to recognize when someone's words or something just didn't ring true, an alert that I might have missed prior to praying this way. Binding myself to God's truth did not mean that I suddenly knew more truth; I just began to sense when things weren't right, even though they looked fine in the natural.

I am now much better about recognizing how important it is to just stand when I do not have a clear direction or leading from the Father. God is never rushed or hurried about what He wants. If you miss a window of opportunity because you were too cautious about wanting to hear from Him, He will open another window for you. If you blow an opportunity because you leaped before you heard Him say NOW, then you may have to walk out some consequences and learn from them. But that opportunity will come back to you if it is part of your destiny.

> God operates outside the realm of time as we know it—He operates in eternity.

Just know this: God is never in a hurry, and He will bless your concern about not wanting to move ahead of Him. Just don't let your concern become a type of quicksand to you—forever holding you in the grip of a fear of moving ahead of God's timing. If you think you might be doing this in some area, then bind your will to His will and bind your timing to His timing. Loose fearful thoughts and wrong patterns of thinking about working together with your heavenly Father.

As you go about your day in the world, you can become overwhelmed with words, sounds, responsibilities, deadlines, and stress. Don't ever forget that you are in this world to influence this age and to bear fruit for the Kingdom of God.

Remind yourself that you are not to be overwhelmed and influenced by the world. You have been given the Keys of the Kingdom to help you do this. Look at what Romans 5:8-10 (TM) says about you and me:

> "God put his love on the line for us by offering his Son in sacrificial death while we were of no use whatever to him. Now that we are set right with God by means of this sacrificial death, the consummate blood sacrifice, there is no longer a question of being at odds with God in any way. If, when we were at our worst, we were put on friendly terms with God by the sacrificial death of his Son, now that we're at our best, just think of how our lives will expand and deepen by means of his resurrection life!"

A Steadied Mind

I heard an interesting expression recently when ministering in a prison. One inmate told me that she finally told someone, "Don't be running your stuff on me!" My mind had been running its stuff on me my whole life. This kept going on until about 1986, when I first began to use the binding and loosing prayers on my own soul. It is comforting to know I can shut down my soul's "stuff" anytime I want to. The one small glitch that can occur is that I have to want to shut it down—I have to make a choice to pray the prayers to stop it.

I had a very strict father who would never allow me to talk back to him, or to even express my feelings about something he had just told me wasn't going to happen. As an only child with no one to talk to, I learned to stuff my anger and sense of injustice. That didn't make the toxic anger go away, it just put it in a pressure cooker. Rage is what anger becomes in a pressure cooker.

Unfortunately, whenever I got into a situation or position that pressured my unsurrendered soul, which tried to keep the lid on the now pressurized anger and rage, my soul would spit up some of its toxic waste. I really didn't know what might spill out of my mouth when I was under too much pressure, and this didn't stop after I became a Christian.

I really struggled to control these old thought patterns when I was around my Christian brothers and sisters. I'm sorry to say that I didn't try so hard when I was out in the world. It still doesn't take too much for opinions on some other driver's driving to spill out of my mouth when they are driving badly.

> I don't have a Christian fish on my car because one of my weak points (or hot spots!) is a teensy, weensy bit of road rage.

In the not too distant past, as the words spilled out, my emotions would kick up and I was looking over the edge of reason into a ravine of road rage.

One day (a few years ago) I saw a very large pickup truck shove a small Toyota right off the road when the young lady driving it wouldn't let him push his way into her lane. He physically moved up against her car and forced her off the road to get right in front of me! The young woman appeared to be all right although she looked like she was in tears as her car sat in the ditch beside the road.

I whipped out my cell phone and dialed 911 and promptly began to chase this bully down the road. I was furious at what he had done. He looked into his rear view mirror and saw me on my cell phone, and he punched his gas pedal. We were off and running! Suddenly the little voice that I hear in my head when God wants my attention said, "Look at your gas gauge." I looked and to my dismay, it was on empty.

I had to pull off and find a gas station, and this bully was going to get away! I was really upset, but there wasn't anything I could do about it. Then I heard the little voice again, and it said, "What did you think you were going to do with him when you caught him?" I realized I hadn't thought that far ahead. I didn't have a clue what I thought was going to do if I caught him. Slowly reason began to try to establish itself in my mind again as I drove on home.

I have to admit that I still talk to other cars around me when I'm driving, but I don't chase them anymore. Really, I don't. One of the things that I have not yet given up is when I am waiting behind a long line of traffic at a stop light. When the light turns green, the cars begin to crawl forward one turtle at a time. I'm usually sitting about eight cars back proclaiming loudly, "Green means GO, you guys. Green means GO. Hello?"

Then one day, I stopped and bound my mind to the mind of Christ as I sat waiting, and something occurred to me. When you bind your time to the timing of God, He may well put delays into your day to keep you on track with arriving safely at your appointed destination. This also effectively keeps you from arriving in the middle of an accident that you might have been a part of!

I am so glad, thrilled even, that I now know I can pray and bind my mind to the mind of Christ—and I can begin to receive His help in bringing my thoughts into captivity.

We read in Philippians 2:5 (KJV), *"Let this mind be in you, which was also in Christ Jesus."*

And we read in 1 Corinthians 2:16 (KJV), " ... *we have the mind of Christ.*"

I kept working with that truth to calm my hot-headed soul. I later realized that binding my mind to the mind of Christ would help me know His thoughts for any situation I might get into, even helping me to pre-empt my soul's loss of control in situations I had not yet encountered.

How do you pre-empt your soul's loss of control? Pray this prayer every morning:

> Jesus, I don't want to do anything today that you wouldn't do. I'm still working with a hot-headed soul that doesn't always share this point of view. But your keys can help me pre-empt its reactions. I bind my mind to your mind, Jesus. I want to hear your voice today as I run into difficult situations. I loose wrong patterns of thinking and wrong attitudes that may try to come up into my consciousness today. I loose the works of the enemy from myself as I go through this day. Help me practice the fruit of patience today, and help me to act as you would in every delay, in every angry look, and with every hard word that may be spoken to me. Let me influence those around me today, passing on your peace and your love. Amen.

These prayers work! This is the true test of a message—does it work? Does it produce positive spiritual results and spiritual fruit? Will it still work in ten years? Twenty years? I can answer those questions with a firm yes. Many who have moving in the message for the past nineteen years or less with lasting change resulting in their lives say they can't imagine not praying the binding and loosing prayers. I have been praying the prayers since 1985 myself, and I've had people from my past say to me, "Who are you, and what have you done with Liberty?"

One More Look at Divine Assistance in a Chemical Library

This story is from the original *Shattering Your Strongholds*, but I want to revisit it here. In approximately 1989, I received one of the strangest consulting jobs I ever experienced—the creation of a paper mill's environmental engineering resource library with an electronic filing system. I was given a computer with a MS-DOS system (thank you, Jesus, for 2005 laptop technology!) and then shown an empty-shelved library filled with boxes of technical books with titles I couldn't even pronounce.

I sat down on the floor in the middle of all those boxes and began binding my mind to the mind of Christ while claiming the Word that says I could do all things through Jesus Christ, which strengthened me. I prayed this over and over with my eyes closed, my head bowed, and my back to the door. I was hoping to give the appearance that I was studying the books in my lap.

To my amazement, as I prayed, my mind began to slowly formulate a logical way to categorize these "foreign language" titles by chemicals, processes, environmental studies, and other areas. I believe Christ's mind, by the Holy Spirit, was feeding supernatural input into my mind. That beginning quickly progressed into a successful completion of a corporate-level research library. In the natural, there was no way I could have organized that material. Jesus had proven himself faithful when I bound my mind to His believing that He would give me help.

I have had people come up to me at meetings to tell me how they identified with this story. One woman even said that this story caused her to believe that if God would do that for me because of the binding and loosing prayers, then God would do it for her. She has become a staunch supporter of this message ever since.

Another word meaning bind also means to compact (*sumbiazo* in the Greek) as used in Ephesians 4:16 (KJV):

> *"From whom (Christ) the whole body fitly joined together and compacted (bound together) by that which every joint supplieth, according to the effectual working in the measure of every part, maketh increase of the body unto the edifying of itself in love."*

Thayer's Greek-English Lexicon of The New Testament describes the word "compacted" as used here to mean, "to cause to coalesce, to join together, put together into one whole." What a beautiful and very practical word for our daily circumstances. Most everyone has had an overload of responsibilities, which seemed to cause their peace to splinter into little pieces. When this happens to me, I stop, drop, and roll—I mean bind! If it works for Smokey the Bear, it will work for me. Things always seem to start moving into position when I do this with focus and clarity.

I know the Holy Spirit certainly caused my "library dilemma" to coalesce and come together into one whole as I bound my mind to the mind of Jesus Christ. I realized from that point on that binding my mind to Christ's mind was a powerful key in situations where I did not know what was going on—situations where I did not know how to meet either the revealed or the hidden expectations of others. Binding prayers snug me up close and personal with God, and I feel strengthened and stabilized by Him every time.

911 Emergency

Another story from my first book has to do with calming serious fear in a crisis situation. I had flown to another city to do some interviews, and someone insisted that an evangelist tell me her 911 story. One night a man's voice insisted she open the door at once for the police. She refused. Through the peephole in her door, she saw what could be a badge, but she was not certain it was. As she argued with them, the men informed her they were about to break down the door.

She ran to the phone, dialed 911, and reported the scenario. To her surprise, the operator informed her the police were indeed at her door and would break it down if she did not let them in at once. When she did, the police entered and soon realized they had made a mistake in seeking a fugitive in the area. They apologized and left. The evangelist sought the Lord for a message about the world's natural 911 and the believer's spiritual Psalms 91:1 (AMP):

> *"He who dwells in the secret place of the Most High shall remain stable and fixed under the shadow of the Almighty (Whose power no foe can withstand)."*

After flying home, I told this story to anyone who would listen. Others found the story interesting, but no one reacted as I did. I even repeated the testimony in my church on the following Sunday night. Again, no one seemed to be particularly impressed. Then four nights later, I was startled awake at 3:00 in the morning by a knocking on my front door. I walked into my living room and called out, "Who is it?"

The reply came, "Open the door; it's the police."

I quickly looked through the peephole and saw total darkness. Assuming someone had their finger over the peephole, I said, "Get your finger off the peephole! I'm not opening this door until I can see you."

A male voice whispered loudly, "We had to remove your porch light for cover. Open the door; this is a life-and-death situation."

"I don't know who you are, and I'm not opening this door!" I hissed back.

A small light clicked on to shine upon something that might have been a badge, but I couldn't be sure. But in its limited reflection, I could see what appeared to be several black ski masks. I yelled through the door, "I can't tell what that says and you don't look like policemen. I'm not opening this door!"

An urgent male voice quickly replied, "That's because we're SERT officers (Special Emergency Response Team, I later learned). This could be a life-and-death situation. Please open the door!"

Sometimes I am a little slow, but finally I began to realize I had heard what was being said once before—in fact, quite recently! "911!" I yelled. "I'm going to call 911."

A muffled voice came back through the door, "Please do, ma'am."

I ran across the living room to punch 911 into my telephone, all the while quoting my spiritual 91:1, "I dwell and abide under the shadow of the Almighty—I'm fixed and stable.

Thank you, Jesus!" I was quickly informed by the 911 operator that it was SERT officers at my front door and it was a life-and-death situation. The SERT officers

> I returned to the door and threw it open to have five masked SERT officers stream into my living room.

were completely outfitted in black from their full coverage masks to their boots. These strange figures carried bullet-proof riot shields, what appeared to be sawed-off shotguns, and black two-way radios.

I was unusually stable and fixed (Psalm 91:1, AMP), a fact I did not realize as remarkable until much later. I calmly asked, "What's going on?"

One team member tersely informed me an armed robber was hiding in the unoccupied house next door to mine. My house was needed for the SERT officers and police negotiators to access my side yard to use their bullhorns to convince the armed man to come out and surrender. The leader said, "We have everything fully covered. We want you to stay on the other side of your house. I don't suppose you could just go back to bed, could you?"

"You're kidding, right?" I said, laughing.

When he then told me that my front door and side door would have to remain open for their access, I stopped laughing and indicated a concern that the robber might get into my house. The team leader said, "Ma am, look out any of your windows."

My house was surrounded with men in camouflage suits training rifles on the house in question. So, I heated some instant coffee in the microwave and went back to my bedroom to read my Bible, pray for everyone involved, and telephone my mother with the exciting news. Instead of a terror-filled experience, the Lord had prepared me, stabilized me, and was about to use me in a unique opportunity.

Before I was finally allowed to leave my home nearly nine hours later, I was telephoned by a local radio station where my mother and my son worked. I was interviewed on the air live, giving a brief testimony about what had preceded my involvement in the current situation. Thousands of people getting ready for work or driving on the freeway that morning heard my spiritual "911" testimony.

Prior to having acquired this new stability (stabilized ability) to know that God's hand is in every situation I walk into, I can't even imagine how I would have reacted before. I was alone in my house with masked men all dressed in black outside my front door demanding entrance to my home at 3:00 in the morning right after they had just deactivated my porch light. That did not fit my early-morning routine! But I am more sure than ever that God is always with me in every situation of my life. Pray this prayer:

I bind myself to you, Lord, because I want to always be stable and fixed in your shadow. I choose to get as up-close-and-personal with you as I can. I bind my thoughts to the mind of Christ so that I can learn to think as He would have me to think. I loose all fearful thoughts about what situations I might end up in this day. It doesn't matter where I go today as long as I am going in your will. I know that you are right there with me. I loose any works of the enemy off myself; I will not allow his tricks to frighten me anymore. Thank you, Father God, for always keeping me safe. Amen.

Right Thoughts/Wrong Spirits—Something Has To Go

I do not find any scriptural reference to Jesus or any of His disciples instructing us to name, speak to, or bind evil spirits. Jesus and His disciples rebuked them as unclean or foul and commanded them to leave. I do believe that evil and demonic spirits exist; I just don't deal with them in the ways I have been previously taught.

We need to recognize the different works of the Holy Spirit, evil spirits, and human souls—which is not as easy as you might think. A seemingly spiritual manifestation that has a clever human soul or an evil spirit behind it can deceive the smartest human intellect.

Amazingly, your soul's cooperation is vital to the operation of the gifts of the Spirit (1 Corinthians 12). If your unsurrendered soul is cluttered with rubbish and residue of past experiences, the spiritual gift of the discerning of spirits cannot flow through you. That leaves you with your own natural wisdom, which is a very bad judge of the difference between a manifestation of the Spirit, an evil spirit, or a human soul.

I have been a Christian since 1972, and I have seen much confusion over the issue of the effects of the works of spirits. All too often believers blame whatever appears to be wrong on Satan or one of his evil spirits. The lack of discernment of spirits can cause believers to deny their own culpability in a situation. It is also very tempting to believe an evil spirit is behind a situation rather than acknowledging a manifestation of ugliness from our own human soul.

When the gift of the discerning of spirits is not active in a believer, that believer can actually fight against a preventative work of the Holy Spirit, believing that he or she is being withheld from important goals by Satan. This is a very dangerous error. It is only by grace that many of us have not been toasted by such behavior because of our arrogance and ignorance.

Satan works through human souls to accomplish his goals. He uses deception and suggestion to plant carnal ideas into the mind, and he sets up situations that play upon wrong beliefs and ideas believers already have stored in their minds. Believers need to recognize that they can align their minds with the mind of Christ, and that they can close the doors Satan would access through their stronghold thinking. This would straighten out a lot of our fights with the devil.

A person who believes that he or she always perceives other peoples' actions and comments as attacks and offenses will sense new affronts and attacks even when they don't exist. Satan is quite capable of maneuvering people around this person to say things that track right with that person's wrong perceptions. You will never be able to control what other people may say to you, but you can loose any wrong perceptions you may have of what others say to you. When you do that, you remove any the "landing strip" for incoming attacks and offenses.

A person who has learned to believe he or she is sickly and weak will not resist coming into agreement with the enemy's efforts to inflict infirmity upon them. Wrong agreements always allow the enemy to inflict his powers of darkness upon those making the wrong agreements. It would be helpful for this person to loose all generational bondage thinking that he has learned from other family members about being sick.

The answer to such spiritual attacks will only be temporary when you focus all your energy and prayers upon fighting with

Satan. The permanent answer lies in dismantling the wrong beliefs and ideas you have along with any stronghold thinking you have put in place to validate them. You do not need to know the source of your wrong thinking. That is one of the best things about praying the binding and loosing prayers. I use an analogy of walking out of a swamp to suddenly realize that you have blood-sucking leeches all over your legs from the knees down. You don't need to know the source of the leeches, their species, or how they attach themselves to your legs—you just need to strip them off of yourself.

This same analogy applies to wrong thinking and to stronghold thinking. If they are in your soul, just strip them out with the loosing prayers. Pray this prayer:

> Lord, I'm tired of always jumping to the wrong conclusions about what people say to me. I'm tired of always giving in to symptoms of colds and the flu. I bind myself body, soul, and spirit to you and your plans and purposes for my life. I loose all patterns of wrong thinking and deceptions that I have bought into. I loose the effects and influences of all wrong agreements I have ever entered into. I loose all generational bondage thinking, religious bondage thinking, and cultural bondage thinking from my soul. Thank you for giving me the Keys of the Kingdom to do this. Amen.

If the thousands of Christians who have tried to bind Satan in chains according to their understanding of Matthew 16:19 had been successful, he wouldn't still be running loose. The right of chaining him up is reserved for the angel who will cast him into the bottomless pit and shut him up for a thousand years as prophesied in the Book of Revelation.

There is more power in doing what Jesus did—He used the truth of the Word of God to counter Satan's deceptions and then He destroyed his works through speaking and praying the Word. He left you with the same power—He left you the Keys of the Kingdom.

Summary

1. The Keys of the Kingdom prayers allow you to be the point of agreement on earth with whatever God has determined His will should accomplish.

2. When you pray for others to cause things in their lives to agree with what the Father has already established in heaven, the Father always does what is best for everyone.

3. The Keys of the Kingdom prayer principles will not get you what *you think you need* unless that is the same thing the *Father knows you need* to walk out your destiny purposes.

4. These prayer keys allow you to come into agreement with God regarding your life and the lives of others to bring about a manifestation of His will.

5. These prayers seek for God's will, Christ's thoughts, and the Holy Spirit's healing comfort in each situation you apply them to.

6. God is never in a hurry, and He will bless your concerns about being careful to not move ahead of Him.

7. Don't ever forget that you are in this world to influence this age and to bear fruit for the Kingdom of God.

8. These prayers work! This is the true test of a message—does it work?

9. A seemingly spiritual manifestation that has a clever human soul or an evil spirit behind it can deceive the smartest human intellect.

10. Lack of discernment of spirits can cause believers to deny their own culpability in a situation.
11. You do not need to know the source of your wrong thinking to loose it.
12. If the thousands of Christians who have tried to bind Satan in chains according to their understanding of Matthew 16:19 had been successful, he wouldn't still be running loose.

Chapter 5

Kingdom Key of Loosing

The Power of Loosing

Many in the Church have been taught to "loose" ministering spirits and the Holy Spirit—believing they were dispatching them to help with troubled situations. In *Thayer's Greek-English Lexicon of the New Testament*, the word "loose" means to crush, smash, and destroy. This is not anything we would want to do to angels or the Holy Spirit (but fortunately we cannot). It is unclear when the Church first began to believe it could dispatch angels or the Holy Spirit to go anywhere, because there is nothing stating that this is possible in any Bible version.

When you speak the word "loose" in your prayers, you are enacting a powerful slashing, smashing, and stripping kind of action. When you pray with the loosing key, you are enacting:

- Shattering stronghold thinking
- Smashing and slashing deception
- Self-surgery
- Spiritual warfare

In the original Greek manuscripts, the word "loose" (together with its root words) means to crush, smash, destroy, dissolve, crack to sunder by separation of the parts, shatter into minute fragments, disrupt, lacerate, convulse with spasms, break forth, burst, and tear apart whatever does not belong in your mind, will, and emotions—or in the souls of those you pray for.

Praying to loose and shatter stronghold thinking means that you can bring the supernatural power of these Keys of the Kingdom words against your soul's stronghold building efforts. Since strongholds are constructed of your soul's skewed logic, reasonings, rationalizations, and justifications, it is comforting to know that you can dismantle these building materials.

> You can loose, smash, crush, and destroy all of the bad attitudes and wrong patterns of thinking that make up the doors, the walls, and the back porch of such a fortress of the mind.

Praying to loose and dissolve deception lodged in your soul brings supernatural power against the lies your soul has bought into and moved into—exposing them to the Son. The word picture here is when you turn an old board over out in a field and all those pale ugly crawly things freak out when the sun hits them.

Without this powerful prayer key, it might take months or even years for truth to break through your strongholds to finally dislodge a lie that has been embraced by your soul. Loosing deception exposes it, allowing you to replace it with truth. You use the keys to make room for truth to move in and take up residence. But loosing wrong things is not the end of the process—it is the beginning of moving right things into your soul to occupy the space created by the loosing prayers.

Self-surgery—now that's an interesting phrase. Think of what God said to His people in Deuteronomy 10:16 (TM):

> *"So cut away the thick calluses from your heart and stop being so willfully hardheaded."*

At other times in the Old Testament, God has said He would cut them away himself, but I would rather do my own cutting if I have a choice. I would especially like to attempt self-removal with the powerful key of loosing that Jesus left for me to use. Remember that loose also means to dissolve, a more comforting thought than having calluses cut off your heart by God. It is a good thing to cooperate with what God wants rather than having God operate on you without your cooperation.

Using the key of loosing in spiritual warfare is a new concept to those who have been taught to bind up Satan and his evil spirits. It's always been somewhat of mystery to me as to what you were going to do with him after you had him bound up. If you have effectively bound him, then he is not going to be capable of taking himself off anywhere such as going back to his domain in hell. And if you just continue to battle evil spirits by binding them, won't you soon be shoulder deep in bound demons?

Jesus did not come to tie up Satan; He came to "destroy" his works (1 John 3:8). The word destroy as used in this verse in the *King James Version* is from the Greek word *luo*, as is the word loose in Matthew 16:19. See how the *Amplified Bible* translates 1 John 3:8:

> *"The reason the Son of God was made manifest (visible) was to undo (destroy, loosen, and dissolve) the works the devil [has done]."*

Jesus did not come to bind up Satan or to destroy him—He came to destroy the works Satan puts into place in our lives, our family's lives, our friend's lives, and the lives of those in the whole world. Someone has to speak loosing prayers of agreement with this, agreement that will tie into God's will in heaven about this. Jesus left works for us to finish after He returned to His Father. Destroying Satan's works is a large portion of the works we should be doing—the remaining portion is that we are to influence the age in which we live by bearing fruit.

Satan's full story has not been played out, as he plays a role in the Book of Revelation. However, you can undo, destroy, loosen, and dissolve his works in human souls in this age in which you live—starting today.

Using the Loosing Key

When you first begin to pray to strip wrong things out of your own unsurrendered soul, begin by loosing these:

1. Wrong beliefs
2. Wrong ideas
3. Wrong attitudes
4. Wrong patterns of thinking
5. Wrong mind sets
6. Stronghold thinking
7. The effects and influences of wrong agreements
8. Preconceived ideas and misconceptions that you have about God, yourself, and others

A word of caution so you won't be surprised later—using this powerful key to dismantle all of the walls and hindrances and blocks in your soul may not be a smooth and easy ride.

We get many calls, letters, and e-mails from new readers who have begun to pray the binding and loosing prayers. Some are thrilled with the answers they are getting, while others are in a full blown state of panic saying:

"I've been binding myself to the will of God and loosing wrong patterns of thinking. Everything imaginable seems to have broken loose in my life. What am I doing wrong?" Or, "Does everybody fall apart after they start praying these prayers?' Or, "I don't like myself anymore since I've been praying those prayers. Aren't the prayers supposed to make me feel better?" Or even this, "I just wanted to tell you that I think those prayers must be of the devil. I feel like I'm losing my mind since I started praying them. I just feel completely out of control. That can't be God ... can it?"

Our standard reply is, "This is perfectly normal, and you're doing fine. Just don't stop praying the prayers, or your soul will gather its wits about it and send the storm troopers to try to get its control back again. It will immediately begin to build its walls back up even higher!"

Why do the prayers seem to cause so much shaking and rocking in the lives of those who pray them? Because divine restoration and renovation are in progress.

> Your soul may feel like it is in the direct path of that wrecking ball many times before it's over.

Think about what happens when a city decides that it has to begin working on its urban renewal projects. Urban renewal is the restoring and cleaning up of the inner parts of the city that have begun to get seedy, dirty, and even dangerous. Lots of old buildings may have to come down, which requires a wrecking ball and maybe even dynamite.

When you begin to initiate urban renewal in your own soul, all of its ratty old shacks and dirty brick fortresses have to be smashed, blown up, or brought down. Its self-centered playgrounds have to be ripped up. Its chain link fences have to be pulled down, and there will be rubble everywhere. In a city's urban renewal, the construction workers can't work with rubble all around them, so the big dump trucks come in and the big front-end loaders are fired up. These massive front-end loaders scoop up the rubble and dump it into the trucks, which take it away forever.

Once all of the rubble is cleared out, then the renewal part of the restoration can begin.

Big chunks of soulish concrete, soulish chain link fences, and the soulish brick buildings in your mind, will, and emotions have to be loaded up and hauled out to make room for your divine renewal to begin. Renovation and restoration in the construction business are never started until everything that has to go has gone and the foundation for the new building is down to ground zero.

Sometimes chucking up these kinds of big chunks out of your soul can be like a poor cat trying to chuck up the biggest hairball in its life. There's going to be wheezing, sneezing, and coughing before it's all over.

Empty Vessels Hold More

In Second Kings 4, we read about the widow of the prophet who was about to lose her two sons into slavery to satisfy her creditors. The only thing she had in her house was a small jar of oil when she cried out to the prophet Elisha for help. He told her to ask all her neighbors for vessels (KJV) and then lock herself in her house with them and her sons, and begin to pour the small jar of oil into the vessels. Elisha promised it would not stop flowing until all the jars were filled. She would be able to sell the oil, pay off all her debts, and live on what was left over.

The basic root of the word "vessel" means to bring a process to completion, according to the *Theological Workbook of the Old Testament*. The processes, which are brought to an end in any given vessel, may be either positive or negative. Something may be continually added to until it is full or complete, or something may be taken away from until there is nothing left—but the totality of the purpose needs to be achieved.

The prophet's widow's miracle required fully empty vessels that were able to receive as much as they could. The first miracle Jesus ever performed was the turning of the water into the

> What if that woman had not bothered to empty out the vessels before she poured the oil?

wine at the wedding in Cana in John 2:7. Jesus told the servants to take large waterpots (KJV) and fill them to the brim with water, which He then turned into wine for the wedding supper. He filled the empty waterpots with a miracle. But what if those waterpots had been filled with rubble?

In 2 Corinthians 4:7 (TM), we read that the Apostle Paul said this:

> *"If you only look at us, you might well miss the brightness. We carry this precious Message around in the unadorned clay pots* (vessels) *of our ordinary lives. That's to prevent anyone from confusing God's incomparable power with us."*

> When the intent of your prayer is pure and you are
> binding things on earth to God's will, answers will be
> set into motion every time you pray.

We are like these clay pots that are to be filled with the precious message of the Gospel—the Good News, vessels that are meant "to bring a process to completion." Your miracle of receiving from God may be diminished, perhaps completely blocked, because your soul has not been emptied out and made ready to receive. Cooperate with your Father in heaven to complete this process. When the intent of your prayer is pure and you are loosing things on earth that are outside of His will, right consequences will be set into motion every time.

One more time, loosing the protective strongholds around all the rubble of your life (which is harbored in your soul) is not pain-free. Neither is having a baby; I know this because I had three of them (one of them being nine and a half pounds!). I know the process of birthing these babies was painful, but I don't really remember the pain.

This is the way it is when you are walking in new territory with God, trying to bring forth something that is going to powerfully change your life and influence those around you.

The important thing is that you not fear any impending discomfort or pain as you loose the rubble from your life— know that it is clearing your soul down to ground zero for the building of great and mighty things that are so wonderful you can't even imagine what they might be!

Force Your Soul to Part with Its Rubble

It may put up quite a fight, but you can force your soul to give up its junk. The binding and loosing keys have the power to help you accomplish this.

I was an over-achiever most of my life until I finally learned to sort of go with God's flow in the last decade. Yet, in my twenties and thirties before I was saved, an overwhelming sense of inadequacy would always wash over me just as I was about to accomplish something great and good. This feeling, coupled with memories of all of my life's failures, had the power to make me feel that I had somehow just conned everyone into believing I could do what needed to be done. Before this con job could be bexposed, I usually chose to self-destruct. That way no one could expose me.

Being raised in an alcoholic home contributed to these feelings, but I had no idea that I had buried them under so many layers of self-protection that the Holy Spirit couldn't show me the truth about them. Buried painful memories foment and ferment, becoming uglier and uglier—just like a container of sewage that has been buried for some time. Some things sort of disintegrate when they are buried, but bad memories are not in this category!

> When bad memories are buried by the self-defense mechanisms of your soul, they do not lie dormant within your soul. They just become gooey, nasty, toxic waste.

The enemy is very aware of all of the negative circumstances in our lives that continue to cripple our thinking and actions long after they happened. His main course of attack against you and me is to continue to recreate circumstances that reinforce the wrong feelings that have grown out of past events.

When I first learned to pray with the loosing key, I was so excited. I loosed every negative experience I could think of, and I quoted the Scripture that says old things are passed away and I was a new creature now. I felt if I quoted that Scripture enough, the new creature would be a done deal. I had no idea that there was a time of transition between leaving the old creature behind and becoming the new creature experientially—even if I already was the new creature positionally because of my salvation experience.

A boy is positionally a man, but a time of transition has to expire before the boy experiences becoming the man. The boy can't become a man by pretending. I still didn't feel like a new creature, but I forced myself to "pretend" that I was anyway. I so wanted to be that new creature because New Creature wouldn't have any bad memories to worry about. New Creature would have a perfect life. I had not yet learned that you cannot loose, dissolve, or destroy the facts of any of the unpleasant things you have experienced. Still, there is no conflict with this fact and the pending new creature status.

God just wants sons and daughters who have allowed Him to forgive them, clean them up, heal them, restore them, and then turn them into lights sent out to influence the world around them and to bear fruit.

Some go overboard telling everyone about every ugly detail that God has brought them out of. Others want to deny the facts of the ugliness of their pasts—the ugliness of what was done to them and the ugliness of what they had done to themselves and to others. Some seem to believe that their pasts embarrass God. These are the ones who try to practice holy amnesia. That might seem to work for a period of time, but it never heals the pain or brings real freedom.

Besides, if you were able to erase or blot out your past, how would you ever know what Jesus had done for you? How could you ever tell others of God's goodness to heal and restore? What hope of refreshing and renewal could you share with them?

God is not embarrassed about anything in your past. Are you embarrassed for your baby when it messes its diapers? Probably not, because you know that the baby has not yet learned how to cooperate with nice social behavior.

I once heard a pastor say that when his little baby son would toddle up to him with a dirty diaper, he never got mad at him. He would pick him up,

> God gets glory from cleaning sinners up, powdering them with sweet grace, and then showing them off to the rest of the world.

clean him up, and powder him up so he smelled sweet. Then with a hug, he would send him toddling off again. My pastor friend said that this reminded him of how God views our mistakes. Our heavenly Father just picks us up, cleans us up (if we will let Him), and then powders us with grace so that we smell sweet again. Then He hugs us and sends us off on our way. He shows us to the world while He says, "See him? Just look at her! This is how I clean up and take care of my kids. Aren't they something?"

God knows that the worst behaviors in people come out of unrenewed minds, unhealed emotions, and unsurrendered wills. He doesn't want those wrong behaviors to continue, but He is compassionate and patient to help you surrender your way out of them. He keeps speaking to us through the Word, through good preaching and teaching, and through the encouragement of our more mature brothers and sisters in Christ—trying to get our cooperation in the process of walking free of our messes.

Think how many times you may have pulled a child out of the mess he was making and that child didn't want to cooperate with you. Did removing him from the mess stop him from trying to go right back into it again? He probably didn't learn anything from your helpful ways until you involved him in the process of putting things back in order. How much more pleasant it is for both you and God when you willingly surrender to His directions on how to cooperate as He helps you get out of your messes. Then the two of you can begin to put things back in order.

You Can't Loose Facts—You Can Loose Their Baggage

Satan knows every painful thing that ever happened to you. He is always ready to reactivate the pain of those experiences whenever he gets a chance. This is why you have to deactivate the negative baggage of those memories by loosing the pain, the fear, and the shame. This removes the fuel he uses for the blow torch he wants to blast you with.

The facts of bad experiences cannot be loosed, but the baggage those experiences have loaded your memories with can be loosed. Once you have loosed all fear, anger, shame, guilt, and bitterness from your soul's bad memories, God can then begin to neutralize them—turning them into nothing more than a comma in the history book of your life. Just keep loosing the baggage connected with your bad memories until your soul gives up trying to put them back on artificial life support. You will come to a place where you know that you are free.

Always remember to bind yourself to the truth and the will of God before you start with your loosing prayers. This is where

> Always remember to bind yourself to the good things of God before you begin loosing things from your soul. Get your safety belt on!

the stability and fixed trust come in to give you strength. A negative past's only positive function is to be the part of your life that you have learned from and have overcome—your reference point to show what God has done for you so you can show others what He will do for them.

Many Christians do not realize they are adamantly resisting any surrender of their bad memories. They replay their inner tapes of anger and guilt over bad memories, failures, and humiliations like those old eight-track tapes that never stopped. The simplest attempts at binding and loosing could jerk their tape player's plug right out of the socket! The only step the hurting Christian needs to make is to choose to do it and then trust God to bring the healing and freedom.

Our old natures have been fed and nourished by what our souls have accumulated and held onto over our lifetimes—everything ever said about us, taken from us, or done to us has had a part in the condition of our souls. I used to wish desperately for guidelines, keys, or anything to help me know how to *"walk and live habitually in the (Holy) Spirit—responsive to and controlled and guided by the Spirit"* (Galatians 5:16, AMP). I didn't seem to be doing too well in my own will power.

If giving up wrong behaviors is accomplished only through your will power—what do you do when your will falters? Everyone's will can fall into confusion and weakness at one time or another, depending upon the pressure and stress one might be trying to withstand. No matter what wrong behavior you have overcome by the power of your will, the enemy and your unsurrendered soul are always looking for a way to pressure you into revisiting the temporary relief that wrong behavior provided for you at another time.

That temporary relief is sort of like taking a pain pill for a needle sticking in your eye. Any feeling of freedom from the pain gradually ebbs away as the pain killer wears off, and you are still left with the needle in your eye. Relief is only permanent when you begin to loose the wrong things in your soul so that God can heal you. The following gives you an understanding of the basic things to loose in your prayers.

Wrong Attitudes

Attitude usually describes the posture of a body or the expression of a face, which reveals the state of mind of a person. Some of the most obvious attitudes include arrogance, conceit, condescension, self-centeredness, negativity, meanness, and impatience. We have spent our whole lives acquiring various attitudes—some good, but many that are quite destructive to others and ourselves.

> Physical posture may give an indication or warning sign of what is going on in a person's soul as well as being reinforced by the expression of the face.

The only right attitudes we should desire as Christians are attitudes expressed by the fruit of the Spirit as listed in Galatians 5:22, (NIV):

1. Love
2. Joy
3. Peace

4. Patience
5. Kindness
6. Goodness
7. Faithfulness
8. Gentleness
9. Self-control (temperance)

Do you remember seeing these attitudes in people you know? An attitude of love is clearly visible in the face of a new mother holding her baby. The attitude is joy is clearly expressed by a father greeting his son coming home from war. An attitude of peace is recognized in the face and body posture of a person communing with the Lord. The attitudes of patience, kindness, and goodness are all recognized in some of the best teachers of children. An attitude of faithfulness is easy to identify in the actions and facial expressions of an elderly wife lovingly assisting her husband with his walker.

Right attitudes need to replace our wrong attitudes. How do we begin to do this?

Bind your mind to the mind of Christ and loose from your soul all wrong attitudes and the stronghold thinking protecting them. If you are aware of specific wrong attitudes that you struggle with, you can loose them by name: unforgiveness, bitterness, negativity, or impatience for example. As you begin loosing all wrong attitudes in general, you may find some surprising things surfacing. I did!

Don't stop with just loosing the wrong attitudes. Begin replacing them with right attitudes such as love, joy, or patience. If you are waiting at a traffic light and the cars in front of you fiddle around until the light turns red and you are left to sit through another light change, loose your wrong attitudes of impatience and anger that may spring up. Force yourself to pray for someone in the car next to you; force yourself to consider that slowing down might put you at the right spot at the right time to influence someone for better.

Force yourself to sing or whistle, "Jesus loves me, this I know. He loves you in your red car, too. He loves you in your truck over there. He's here right now, so let's be fair!" It will be hard not to smile if you do that. A smile goes a long way in dissipating a bad mood.

Wrong Patterns of Thinking

The word "pattern" has many meanings, but the one that best describes wrong patterns of thinking is the model used to make a mold into which molten metal is poured to form a casting. This pattern/mold is so rigid, it can actually hold and shape molten metal—that's pretty rigid! Regardless of what you pour into this pattern/mold—liquid gold, molten metal, wet cement, or Jell-O—the end result will come out shaped exactly the same way every time.

When any pattern of thinking gets locked into place in your mind, it becomes a mind set.

Most of us know someone who is so sensitive that he or she is offended by nearly everything that others say. Some people who have never gotten over being mistreated develop patterns of thinking that colors all input from others as abusive. When people feel the need to justify having this pattern of thinking, they build strongholds around it. This provides the devil with opportunities to twist and distort their perceptions further. Some very dangerous personalities having emerged from some of these exact situations—serial killers, rapists, psychotics, etc.

Anyone who has repeatedly been told they are stupid, ugly, worthless, or a failure will invariably develop patterns of wrong thinking about themselves. Those patterns have the power to mold all future input into a negative

> You cannot loose the facts of what has been done to you—but negative, fearful, unhealthy patterns of thinking birthed from those facts can be loosed.

reinforcement of this person's beliefs. The power of these pattern/molds can be so strong that it overrides all truth others may try to share. Some other wrong patterns of thinking include self-hatred, a sense of personal worthlessness, self-deception, and self-destructiveness. Any pattern of thinking that cannot be verified with Christ-like thinking brings defeat.

Traumatic things happen in all of our lives. If the emotional reactions and bad feelings born from such experiences are not released to God, they will cause you rationalize and justify wrong behaviors you use to subdue your bad feelings about the experience. Rationalizing and justifying are two of the planks used in building strongholds to protect your right to think however you want—perpetuating your pain by keeping the traumatic memory locked in and God locked out.

Always remember to use the binding and loosing principles as linked actions. Bind your mind to the mind of Christ to stabilize and steady it, because the act of loosing can cause your soul to search for ways to protect itself. The soul won't care if it causes you more pain or not; it will simply react out of fear when it feels it is losing its defensive mechanisms.

Wrong Ideas

An idea can be described as a concept, an explanation, a plan, or a scheme—something that exists in the mind as a result of mental activity. In other words, your ideas are the representation of your thoughts on a given subject.

The word "idea" is not used in the King James Bible; the closest words used are "thoughts" and "imaginations." In 2 Corinthians 10:45, the Word speaks of the need for casting down evil *imaginations* and every high thing that would raise itself up between you and God. The use of loosing prayers will cast down things in your soul so that you can bring every <u>thought</u> into captivity to the obedience of Christ.

When we pray and loose all wrong ideas from our souls, we are shattering, smashing, and dissolving evil imaginations, wrong theories, reasonings, and thoughts that get in the way of our understanding of God. Loosing is a powerful way to strip wrong ideas out of our unsurrendered souls to make room to understand God.

Wrong Desires

A desire a strong feeling of wanting to have something or wishing for something to happen—a longing or a craving for something or someone that is believed to be able to bring satisfaction or pleasure. A right desire would be wanting a deeper relationship with Jesus Christ. A right desire could be for fellowship or beautiful music. A right desire could be

> Desire in itself is neither right nor wrong; it is the object of the desire that turns it into something good or something evil.

for a marriage, as long as God is allowed to bring the mate and the timing.

Wrong desires and powerful soulish drives are usually connected to covetousness, self-gratification, greed, self-indulgence, or attempts to fill up feelings of emptiness in the soul. Socially unacceptable attempts to get deep inner needs met often bring rebuke and ridicule. The acting out of a need can be perceived and labeled as a weakness of character or a personal fault. This causes the needy person to build strongholds around his needs, hoping to hide them from others.

Sometimes I wish I had a big red bandwagon to get on or a giant soap box in the park where I could use a megaphone to call out: UNMET NEEDS ARE NOT CHARACTER FLAWS—UNMET NEEDS ARE FACTS. An unfilled gas tank is not a flaw in the design of a car; it is a fact. An empty wallet is not a personal failing of your bank; it is a fact. The only way to fix these situations is to fill the need. God is the one who can fill any unmet needs.

Unmet needs that are driven underground in wounded souls do not lie there dormant. They become like demented strains of yeast that cause bread dough to grow and grow, spilling over the confines of a bread pan to flow onto the floor of the kitchen and then to crawl all the way through the house. The bread dough that ate Los Angeles, or something like that.

Wrong desires boil up out of buried, unmet needs with forceful, destructive drives that aggressively demand fulfillment. These drives push the soul to pull the body into wrong mind/body agreements that result in divorce, adultery, stealing, lying, cheating, abuse, and even murder. Loose wrong desires and personal agendas from your soul while also loosing the stronghold thinking that rationalizes and defends them.

Keep tearing away at the defense mechanisms of your soul until you open a way for the Father to pour healing, mercy, and grace into your unmet needs and unhealed hurts. The moment you crack open the door of your soul's inner chambers, He will be there to fix your brokenness.

Wrong Beliefs

A belief is trust and confidence placed in something even if you cannot prove it exists. When you trust in something that you can prove, then you know it exists. If you trust something you cannot prove, you have the faith to believe it exists. Christians have the ability to place their confidence and trust in right beliefs and also in wrong beliefs. Sustained faith in a wrong belief can cause the erecting of a stronghold to prevent others from exposing the deception. This stronghold can be reinforced every time someone tries to counter the wrong belief.

> When wrong beliefs are loosed, they need to be replaced with right beliefs.

Loosing wrong beliefs temporarily displaces them, creating an empty space in your soul. Your soul will soon move to reestablish them unless you fill that space with right beliefs. Bind your mind to the mind of Christ and bind yourself to the truth. Begin to search the Word of God for truths that relate to the wrong beliefs that you are aware that you had. Begin to practice those truths. Keep loosing wrong beliefs you have learned to trust while also loosing deceptions the enemy has convinced you to believe to be true.

Go Where He Wants to Go

Only God is wise enough to know where His plans for your life should take you. Those plans may not include fame or wealth or a certain mate or a certain career, so it is not productive to bind yourself to such plans. The power of the Keys of the Kingdom lies in binding yourself to God's will, obligating yourself to the plans and purposes He has for you.

If you bind yourself to something that is not in God's plans for your future, you won't get it from God. BUT Satan may try to provide it for you just to mess up your ideas of effective prayer. The best plan is to keep your binding prayers as simple as possible—bind your will to God's will, bind your mind to the mind of Christ, and so on.

Also, keep your loosing prayers as simple as possible. I have had many people want me to give them specific loosing prayers so that they can get rid of certain negative things in their lives. I tell them that negative things in our lives are usually the consequences of wrong choices. Then they want to loose the consequences or loose the wrong choices. The human soul always wants to complicate everything.

You cannot loose consequences because the consequences of wrong choices are facts—they are going to show up with a vengeance every time a bad choice is made. I once likened the consequences of wrong choices to a herd of elephants charging right at you from a distance of just six feet away. They are going to get you, no matter what you do.

Instead of trying to loose consequences, the only positive thing you can do when they show up is work

> It won't do any good to loose wrong choices, because making right choices must be learned through practice.

very hard to learn from them so you don't have to go through them again (and again). You can't loose bad piano playing to become a concert pianist—you have to practice playing the piano in a right way to stop being a bad player. You can loose wrong patterns of thinking and wrong beliefs you have about making choices, but you still need to practice making right choices.

Sticking to these guidelines, I am finding it easier to not get into conflict with His will or the plan He is unfolding for me—which obviously is the best place to be.

The Book That Wouldn't Go Away

God has brought opportunities and blessings to me that I never even dreamed about when I began my relationship with Jesus. My first book *Shattering Your Strongholds* was written in 1992, and I am still amazed at what God continues to surprise me with as I keep binding my will to His will, while loosing all wrong thinking and the works of the enemy from my soul.

We are in contact with many who have been using the Keys of the Kingdom prayer principles for years. Their lives have changed dramatically and their relationships have been immensely improved. We have also heard from some who used the principles for awhile and then decided they didn't want to use them anymore. This is always sad because it means that their souls got them back under control again. I am delighted when people come up and tell me that although they read the book years ago and gave up—now they have reread the book, are praying the prayers, and things are happening!

One lady who had lived with a motorcycle gang sat through my first training classes in 1992 before my first book had even been released. She didn't get the book until just before she finished the tenth class. I never saw her again.

Then in 2002, ten years later, she wrote to me saying: "I hated your book *Shattering Your Strongholds*. I used to throw it across the room and scream how stupid it was. I tried to throw it away, and I tried to lose it every time I moved. But that stupid book just wouldn't go away! Well, I've reread it now, it's not stupid, and I'm praying the prayers. My life has turned around completely, I'm going to college to be a nurse, and I am doing well. Thanks so much."

When you are able to communicate with a certain amount of excitement, it is not that unusual to find somebody who gets what you are sharing. This is <u>not</u> the true test of a Kingdom message. The true test of a Kingdom message is whether or not the hearer is still rejoicing, growing, and moving in the truth several years later. The true test is whether or not that person is beginning to influence the age in which they live and whether they have borne any fruit.

The true test is whether or not they finally pick THE BOOK THAT WOULD NOT GO AWAY back up ten years later and are growing and moving in God's truth!

Summary

1. Praying to loose and shatter stronghold thinking means that you can bring the supernatural power of these Keys of the Kingdom words against your soul's stronghold building efforts.

BEYOND Shattered Strongholds

2. Loosing deception exposes it, allowing you to replace it with truth. You use the keys to make room for truth to move in and take up residence.

3. Destroying Satan's works is a large portion of the work we should be doing—the remaining portion is that we are to influence the age in which we live and to bear fruit for the Kingdom of God.

4. Your soul may put up quite a fight, but you can force it to give up its junk. The binding and loosing keys have supernatural power to help you accomplish this.

5. The facts of bad experiences cannot be loosed, but the baggage those experiences have loaded your memories with can be loosed.

6. Always remember to bind yourself to the truth and the will of God before you start with your loosing prayers.

7. Relief from fears and doubts becomes permanent when you create room in your soul so that God can heal you.

8. When any pattern of thinking gets locked into place in your mind, it becomes a mind set.

9. Any pattern of thinking that cannot be verified with Christ-like thinking brings defeat.

10. Always remember to use the binding and loosing principles as a linked action.

11. Loosing is a powerful way to strip wrong ideas out of our unsurrendered souls to make room to understand God.

12. UNMET NEEDS ARE NOT CHARACTER FLAWS—UNMET NEEDS ARE FACTS.

Chapter 6

The Power of Forgiveness

The Dungeon

I have always loved certain comic strips and one of my favorites is "Rose is a Rose" by Pat Brady, a Christian cartoon artist. His comic strips are about a family: Sweet Jimbo; the usually sweet Rose; Rose's alter ego with an attitude who is named Vicki (who rides a Harley and likes rattlesnake chili); their young son, Pasquale; Pasquale's guardian angel (sometimes a small version of Pasquale with little wings and other times a huge warrior angel with sword and shield); and their cat, Peekaboo. Yes, I really, really like this cartoon!

One of the my favorite scenarios is when Rose is plunged into a dungeon because she is angry at Jimbo and doesn't want to

> Unforgiveness will eventually land you in a dungeon of your own dark, ugly thoughts.

forgive him. Forgiving is the only way she can get out of the dark, dank dungeon of her own soul's unforgiveness—and she doesn't always want to pay the price for her freedom. However, Rose always forgives within a day or two, and then she's up and out of the dungeon.

Forgiveness is your soul's get-out-of-jail/dungeon-free card, too.

True forgiveness means you give up any claim you have against another person for an offense they have committed. Forgiveness is an act of granting a full pardon without harboring any resentment towards the offender. Not harboring any resentment is the final phase of forgiveness—without it, the forgiveness is false. If you believe you have forgiven someone, but you still feel a bit itchy or twitchy towards them at times, you need to ask God to show you just how true your forgiveness is.

Forgiving is definitely an eternal matter that must be settled here on earth. The Bible has much to say about forgiveness:

> *"And forgive us our debts, as we forgive our debtors.. .. For if ye forgive men their trespasses, your heavenly Father will also forgive you; but if ye forgive not men their trespasses, neither will your Father forgive your trespasses." Matthew 6:12,14-15 (KJV)*

> *"And when you stand praying, if you hold anything against anyone, forgive him, so that your Father in heaven may forgive you your sins." Mark 11:25 (NIV)*

> *"And be ye kind one to another, tenderhearted, forgiving one another, even as God for Christ's sake hath forgiven you." Ephesians 4:32 (KJV)*

> *"Bear with each other and forgive whatever grievances you may have against one another. Forgive as the Lord forgave you." Colossians 3:13 (NIV)*

These verses seem to clearly say that we will receive God's forgiveness in exactly the same manner that we offer forgiveness to others. When you have rationalized and justified feelings of unforgiveness, then you not only have the dungeon factor to deal with, you have stronghold thinking involved, too. When strongholds are involved, forgiveness can be very difficult.

Yet forgiving unconditionally brings an incredible reward, which cannot be acquired any other way. This reward is TOTAL FREEDOM from:

- Responding to
- Reacting to and
- Replaying

old offenses and hurts that still seem so alive sometimes. Forgiveness sucks all the life right out of them.

Still, some believe having to forgive everyone for everything unconditionally, all the time is an impossible condition to meet—even if it is the ultimate criteria required to assure their own forgiveness. These people doggedly cling to their rationalizations and justifications that the other person should be punished in some way. In Romans 12:19 (TM), we read what Paul told the Roman Christians about God's words on getting even:

> "Don't insist on getting even; that's not for you to do. 'I'll do the judging,' says God. 'I'll take care of it.'"

True forgiveness means that you will give up all resentment, all desire to get even, and you will completely annul and make void

Getting even almost seems hard-wired into so many people today.

139

whatever has been done to you, said to you, or taken from you. This probably seems like an impossible sacrifice for some unsurrendered souls. But there are times when God asks us to simply give up our human understanding of our so-called human rights.

We must realize that God's viewpoint and our viewpoints aren't even on the same planet sometimes, but He is God and He is good and fair.

Personal Experience with Offenses

When God asks you to do something that you are convinced you cannot do, know that He never asks you to do anything that is impossible for you to do. If He says you are to forgive, He knows that you can do it. And you can forgive the worst offense ever when you use the binding and loosing prayers to knock the rigidity and rebellion out of your soul.

How do you really test a new spiritual theory like this? The best way to prove that these prayers work is not by praying them when you are comfortable and happy. Pray these prayers when you are angry, when you are fearful, when you are under extreme stress—this is how you will prove that they work. This way of praying is not just for the little daily irritations you face—this way of praying can also move big dark mountains of unforgiveness out of your soul!

I've been saved since 1972. I had very little trouble forgiving other Christians after I got saved, probably because I denied that any hard things existed while I tripped about forgiving as many easy things as I could. "You took the pew I always sit in? That's okay, I forgive you." "You didn't show up for coffee this morning like you said you would? That's okay, I forgive you." I was in denial for years that there some big ugly offenses fomenting and fermenting in my unsurrendered soul.

I spoke with a pastor one day about offenses and how hard it seemed for so many to just forgive the people who offended them. This pastor told me of a children's book that she uses when counseling adults about their unforgiveness issues. She said that the book's protagonist was a little boy who had been offended by something his sister said to him. As the little boy walked angrily away from his sister, a small fuzzy creature stepped up to take his hand and walk with him. The little creature's name was Offense, and it sympathized with the little boy and patted his shoulder consolingly.

Then the story evolved into the little creature Offense being replaced by a larger unattractive creature who began to lead the boy down the path they were walking. This creature's name was Unforgiveness. Then the story evolved into a third creature that replaced Unforgiveness, a very big, hideous-looking monster. The monster's name was Resentment, and he dragged the little boy wherever he wanted to.

Being a writer, I was delighted with this marvelous analogy that the author had used to teach children how innocent, even self-comforting, unforgiveness can seem to be in its early stages. I think that 99 percent of all adults today could benefit from reading this children's book, too. Offense, Unforgiveness, and Resentment all conspire to lead you away from God and from your destiny purposes as a child of the King of Kings.

The Nuts and Bolts of Forgiveness

First Peter 2:23-24 (AMP) tells us a very graphic story of what happened to our Savior:

> *"When He was reviled and insulted, He did not revile or offer insult in return; when He was abused and suffered, He made no threats of vengeance; but He trusted Himself and everything to Him who judges fairly. He personally bore our sins in His own body to the tree as to an altar and offered Himself on it, that we might die (cease to exist) to sin and live to righteousness. By His wounds you have been healed."*

Jesus was treated very badly during the three years of His ministry on earth. The Sadducees and the Pharisees accused Him of terrible things at every turn. He was beaten and bruised, spit upon, and finally brutally crucified. If He had been offended by these things, He would have never fulfilled His destiny purposes for His Father. But He entrusted everything that happened to Him to His Father who always judges fairly. He held no resentment against those who hurt Him; in fact He said on the cross, *"Father, forgive them, for they know not what they do."*

The Bible says that by His wounds (which went far beyond the little offenses we get so upset about), wounds received at the hands of people who hated Him, we would be forgiven and healed of our wounds received at the hands of others. When we refuse to revile, insult, or threaten vengeance when we are wounded, we allow His wounds to heal us. When we refuse to forgive, His wounds were suffered in vain and we receive no healing for ours.

First Peter 3:9-11 (AMP) reads:

> *"Never return evil for evil or insult for insult— scolding, tongue lashing, berating; but on the contrary blessing—praying for their welfare, happiness and*

protection, and truly pitying and loving them. For know that to this you have been called, that you may yourselves inherit a blessing (from God)—obtain a blessing as heirs, bringing welfare and happiness and protection. For let him who wants to enjoy life and see good days (good whether apparent or not), keep his tongue free from evil, and his lips from guile (treachery, deceit). Let him turn away from wickedness and shun it; and let him do right. Let him search for peace—harmony, undisturbedness from fears, agitating passions and moral conflicts—and seek it eagerly. Do not merely desire peaceful relations (with God, with your fellowmen, and with yourself), but pursue, go after them!"

Hard times, painful times, do happen to Christians. But these times do not have to just be endured; they can become something good in our lives. Going through tribulation with the right attitude can become patience, experience, and hope in our souls (Romans 5:3-4, KJV). The Greek word for "experience" means acceptable, proven, tried, trusted, tested—in other words, character that has been proven. If your character is being proven by difficult experiences, then use the experiences to grow and to give God glory.

I heard someone once liken Romans 8:28 to baking a cake from scratch—I remember thinking that was quite a stretch. Romans 8:28 tell us, "... *we know that all things work together for good to those who love God, to those who are the called according to His purpose*" (NKJV). Think about what you do when you bake a cake from scratch. You line up baking soda, baking power, salt, raw eggs, flour, and flavorings on the counter. All of the ingredients are there, but it is not a cake until the Cook comes and works them together for good.

We often experience baking soda times or raw eggs days. Perhaps we have a week of salt. These times are not pleasant; in fact, it can be very hard to imagine that they could ever enhance our lives. Yet, they are part of the whole cake. The Cook takes all of the things that can be offensive on their own and blends them into a good thing, a very good thing. How wonderful it could be if we could learn to look at the difficult things of our lives as being part of the final good thing that God is blending together.

> The difference between the baking soda, eggs, salt and the finished cake is the Cook.

There must be room in our lives to experience the stages of growth that our faith must go through. Untried, untested, untempered faith is not overcoming faith; it is baby faith. Babies do not understand the purpose of their faith. This may not be the Golden Rule, but it is surely the Silver Rule: *Faith is not given so you can avoid the hard times; it is given to get you **through** the hard times.* Every time you come out on the right end of an offense or a trial, full of faith and forgiveness, you become more like fine gold.

As you pray the prayers of binding and loosing, also pray the words of God like this:

> Father, your Word says that my baking soda times and raw egg days can bring about something positive in me when you are allowed to work them into that good thing. I bind myself to your will in all of my baking powder days. Through them teach me patience, teach me your timing, and help me grow into the spiritual experience I need to become an overcomer. I loose all of the resistance, rigidity, and stubbornness from my soul. I loose all rationalizations and justifications and wrong patterns of thinking that keep me from learning what

you know I need to learn. I want to make room within my soul for the growth of the fruit of your Spirit. Help me to forgive without harboring any resentment. I want to become experienced in the ways of your Spirit. You have promised your hope will sustain me while this is being worked out in me. Amen.

Dealing With Anger

Anger is a powerful, God-given emotion because it is an invaluable component of the passion, courage, and boldness that lie within us to do great and mighty things. Our unsurrendered souls, however, use anger for all the wrong reasons. God meant for our anger to be converted into spiritual energy to bring justice and deliverance to others. Our unsurrendered souls turn anger against other people instead. Anger is never an acceptable response to a personal affront.

There is not one recorded instance in the Bible where Jesus was angry because someone had stepped on His toes or had gotten in the way of His self-desires or self-interests. His anger was only directed against those who wanted to hinder His Father's will and desecrate His Father's house.

Still, God knew there would be times when we would be angry. He warned us through the Apostle Paul about using the anger against other people. Paul wrote to the Ephesian believers (Ephesians 4:26-27, AMP):

> "When angry, do not sin; do not ever let your wrath— your exasperation, your fury or indignation—last until the sun goes down. Leave no such room or foothold for the devil—give no opportunity to him."

In other words, there is a time limit on how long we can take to work through our anger. No matter how we look at the above Scripture, we have less than twenty-four hours to resolve our anger at anyone or anything. If we do not, we become fair game for the enemy to use the opportunity we have given him to establish a foothold in our lives.

This is like a grass fire burning all around an oil well or along a natural gas pipe line.

Soulish anger is usually an emotional reaction to something that has hurt you, confused you, or frightened you. It is a powerful reaction that feeds off of unresolved issues and unhealed hurts in your life. What might start out as just a snit can flare into rage, even a murderous rage, when it feeds on unhealed pain long enough. Soon or later, something is going to explode if the fire is not put out.

Angry feelings have little hair roots that function almost like industrial-strength Velcro, feeding off your unhealed hurts, unresolved issues, and unmet needs. The longer these feelings are allowed to fester, the deeper their roots go. The sooner we loose those kinds of feelings, the better off we are. Such feelings can ride roughshod over our born-again spirit's input. When they do, we have to fight our unsurrendered soul and the devil as we drag ourselves back up the hill to try to hear from God again.

It is far better that you turn to the Word of God as your plumb line for truing up your soul the minute you feel indignant, offended, or wronged. Bind yourself to the will of God; bind your raggedy emotions to the healing balance of the Holy Spirit, and then loose wrong attitudes, wrong patterns of thinking, and any strongholds associated with them. Then pray this prayer, based on the words of Psalms 119:165 and Proverbs 16:18:

"Lord, your Word says if I love you and my soul is full of your words, I will have great peace and nothing shall offend me. I'm pretty offended right now, so I need your help. I bind my will to your will. I bind my mind to the mind of Christ, and I bind my emotions to the healing balance of the Holy Spirit. Your Word says pride goes before destruction and a haughty spirit goes right before a fall. Father, I'm in enough trouble without destruction and a fall coming into my life. I loose all negative feelings that I have against_ _____. Forgive me for having held on to them this long. I choose to forgive _____ right now. Soul, you will forgive this offense and release it forever. Mind, you will not harbor any resentful thoughts or attitudes against _____. Will, you must surrender this whole thing to the Father right now. Emotions, I loose all fear and doubt from you. Thank you, Jesus, for the Keys of the Kingdom that make it possible for me to do this. Amen."

God Hates Pride

The Bible, the dictionaries, and the fathers of the faith have a lot of negative things to say about pride. Pride is described in these ways:

- Inordinate self-esteem
- Having an excessively high opinion of oneself
- Feeling better than others
- Evaluating others in relation to your own feelings of superiority
- Excessive self-promotion
- Conceitedness and egotism
- Unreasonable conceit manifesting itself in contempt of others

• Excessive belief in one's own abilities

Pride is the high opinion that a soul entertains of itself. Pride always attempts to present itself to others in a superior light, and is anxious to gain praise and applause. Pride is often distressed when slighted, and impatient if ignored or contradicted. To be excessively proud of having knowledge, power, influence, or virtue totally negates the value of these achievements in the eyes of God and in the eyes of righteous men and women. Pride is disgraceful to God and it is a barrier to communion with God.

Proverbs 6:16-19 (KJV) begins with this statement, *"These six things doth the Lord hate: yea, seven are an abomination to him ... "* What is at the head of this list of seven things that are an abomination to God? Is it fornication, homosexuality, murder, adultery, blasphemy? No. The list begins with pride. *"These six things doth the Lord hate: yea, seven are an abomination to him:*

1. *A proud look*
2. *A lying tongue*
3. *Hands that shed innocent blood*
4. *A heart that deviseth wicked imaginations*
5. *Feet that be swift in running to mischief*
6. *A false witness that speaketh lies*
7. *He that soweth discord among the brethren."*

Pride is not always an overdeveloped sense of superiority. Sometimes pride is the soul's attempt to make itself feel that it looks better in the eyes of someone who might think it to be inferior. When a soul's pride of self is ignored or contradicted, hurt feelings can abound. Great embarrassment can abound when the soul's self-pride seems to be devalued by others.

Whenever pride, anger, hurt feelings, bitterness, or self-righteousness over being disrespected gets a grip on you, first deal with yourself through the prayers of binding and loosing. Then take the offense to Jesus in words that line up with God's will and His instructions like this:

> In the name of Jesus Christ, I bind my will to your will, Father, and I bind my mind to the mind of Jesus Christ. I loose all of my wrong attitudes that have come out of self-pride. I loose all of my wrong beliefs about how I have been disrespected. Jesus, I repent right now of the sin of anger and pride and wrong thoughts. Please forgive me and wash me clean. Teach me how to be humble, however you have to do it. I thank you that I can come right to the Father's throne with confidence and find mercy and grace to do so. Thank you, Jesus. Amen.

The opposite of pride is humility. Humility is modesty, being unpretentious, and being unassuming in attitude and actions towards other people. Modesty is an attitude of respect and deference for other people's wishes. Humility has no problem with forgiving others. Pride has a lot of trouble with believing it should stoop to forgiving.

Ongoing Discussion about Unforgiveness

I have found that next to stating that Christians cannot have demons in themselves, the second subject that raises a LOT of Christians' hackles is the subject of unforgiveness. I believe that this condensation of many e-mail discussions I have had with people who have disagreed with my understanding of forgiveness will allow me to address some of the viewpoints that keep believers separated on this important subject.

Question: I have recently read both of your books and have been richly blessed. I do have a concern regarding a sentence in SYS. On page 117, you say "that unforgiveness in your heart can send you to hell no matter what else you are doing spiritually right." This is biblically incorrect since salvation is by grace through the acceptance of Jesus and His finished work on the cross and not by our works.

Answer: I have grown in grace since I wrote that in 1990, and I have since realized that truth goes "down" better when it is mixed with grace. However, all the grace in the universe does not change the fact that there will be no unforgiving souls allowed in heaven. When are people going to get around to obeying God's command on forgiveness? As they travel up through the air?

Unforgiveness is disobedience to God and it is sin. If God drove Adam and Eve from His Garden of Eden (earthly Paradise) for the sin of eating a forbidden apple, how could He will welcome someone into His perfect heavenly Paradise with the sin of unforgiveness in their souls? Unforgiveness will not be worked out after we leave this life. It must be worked out here on earth.

Someone once said to me, "What if the rapture was going to occur in five minutes, and I had unforgiveness in my soul? Are you saying that I wouldn't get to go?" I replied that those would probably become the most INTENSE five minutes this person would experience in his entire life, just because God did want him to go!

The Holy Spirit will work and work with believers to help them forgive, dispensing great spiritual and emotional pressure as well as grace upon the soul of the one who keeps refusing. I believe these workings and dealings intensify when the individual continues to resist surrendering his or her unforgiveness.

The Father's purposes for us here on earth *are to conform us to the image of His Christ.* Christ (in the worst possible time frame of His life on earth) offered pure forgiveness, without any casting of judgment, saying about those who were nailing Him to the cross (in Luke 23:34, KJV).

> *"Father, forgive them; for they know not what they do."*

God's whole plan of salvation is based upon the principle of forgiving. God's grace is extended to give us every opportunity to grow in love while we are *"working out our own salvation in fear and trembling,"* as Paul said to the Philippian Christians in Philippians 2:12. Speaking to believers, Paul spoke here of salvation to mean the renewing of the unrenewed mind, the healing of the wounded emotions, and surrendering of the unsurrendered will. These Christians had already experienced the salvation of their spirits.

We cannot renew ourselves; we can only cooperate with God's renewal in us. We cannot heal ourselves; we can only receive the healing grace and mercy of the Holy Spirit's work in us. BUT we can and must surrender our own wills. If, *after intense dealings of the Holy Spirit,* unforgiving individuals still will not forgive—isn't there a question of the motivation of their confession of surrendering their lives to Christ as their Lord and Master?

Accepting Christ is not merely an escape from hell and a defense against the devil. Accepting Christ is a commitment to love, honor, and obey Him as Lord and Master. How can people claim Christ as Lord and Master of their lives and then refuse His command to forgive others? Is it not hypocrisy to expect His forgiveness when you are refusing to forgive another human being?

This issue seems to be very serious to Christ. This is clear in the statement He made after telling the parable of the king and his unforgiving servant in Matthew 18:32-35 (NIV):

> *"Then the master called the servant in. 'You wicked servant,' he said, 'I canceled all that debt of yours because you begged me to. Shouldn't you have had mercy on your fellow servant just as I had on you?' In anger, his master turned him over to the jailers to be tortured, until he should pay back all he owed. This is how my heavenly Father will treat each of you unless you forgive your brother from your heart."*

The term brother used in this verse is not a loophole for only having to forgive a sibling or a fellow Christian. If this verse only referred to forgiving other believers, that would require you to judge a person's spiritual state to determine whether or not you needed to forgive them. We are told that we are not to judge others, lest we be judged ourselves. The issue of your forgiveness of another person has nothing to do with their spiritual state—but it has everything to do with yours!

I don't know of any other sin spoken of so graphically in its consequences (especially in Matthew 18) as this one. There is too much in the Word about forgiveness to ever downplay the issue of forgiving. The Lord's Prayer simply asks the Father to *"forgive us as we forgive others."*

Question: Liberty, your book, *Shattering Your Strongholds*, seems to be a sincere attempt to help people gain freedom from their struggles. You have an interesting view of binding and loosing that is worth considering. However, some of us disagree with your statement on page 117 that "unforgiveness in your heart can send you to hell no matter what else you are doing right. Forgiveness is a matter of eternal life or death." How can a person with your spiritual training and background say such a thing?

Please listen to what I have to say. We are all FOR FORGIVENESS! It's a good and healthy thing to do! Think of all the new believers who have been told that it is okay if they still have anger and bitterness and hatred (all by-products of unforgiveness) in their hearts, God understands why they cannot forgive someone who has hurt them deeply, and that the blood of Christ will cover it. Think of how God must feel about that after He sent His own Son to die to provide their forgiveness.

Answer: I know that my books go against the grain of some of the understanding of the Scriptures on forgiveness today. My writings have never been easy for unsurrendered souls to accept. That is not intentional. But after praying for years and binding myself to the truth while loosing preconceived ideas, wrong teachings of man, and wrong attitudes from my own soul, I have written what I believe to be true.

I am sure you have heard of Matthew Henry's and Adam Clarke's commentaries. Most of the older saints' writings that are preserved for research today show that while they certainly believed in Christ's sacrifice and the grace and mercy that accompanied it, they also believed in all of the Scriptures regarding the eternal importance of forgiveness. Read what Matthew Henry's and Adam Clarke's commentaries have to say about the Lord's Prayer as written in Matthew 6. Forgive me if this sounds immodest, but I think I am in good company here.

"On Matthew 6:12: (Forgive us as we forgive our debtors.) This is not a plea of merit, but a plea of grace. Note, those that come to God for the forgiveness of their sins against him, must make conscience of forgiving those who have offended them, else they curse themselves when they say the Lord's prayer" (from *Matthew Henry's Commentary*).

"On Matthew 6:12: (As we forgive our debtors.) It was a maxim among the ancient Jews that no man should lie down in his bed without forgiving those who had offended him. That man condemns himself to suffer eternal punishment who makes use of this prayer with revenge and hatred in his heart. He who will not attend to a condition so advantageous to himself (remitting a hundred pence to his debtor, that his own creditor may remit him 10,000 talents) is a madman, who, to oblige his neighbor to suffer an hour, is himself determined to suffer everlastingly! This condition of forgiving our neighbor, though it cannot possibly merit anything, yet it is that condition without which God will pardon no man" (from *Adam Clarke's Commentary*).

> **Question:** Dear Liberty, having just received your latest newsletter I find myself deeply dismayed at one of your answers to one of your constituents. I am concerned for you and for the implications your answer may hold for your ministry. It has to do with the question asked by CM and the intensely important issue of salvation. I do know beyond a shadow of a doubt that salvation is by the grace of God in and through Jesus Christ. I believe your response to CM suggests otherwise. Liberty, if the answer you gave to CM is true, I believe that even you yourself would have a difficult time entering into God's holy heaven. Unforgiveness may have never been something they have dealt with consciously before, and something that they may never deal with until they are in the presence of the Lord

in heaven. In such cases it simply cannot "be worked out here, now" as you state. Pastor LB

Answer: There is nothing in the Bible that says that having to forgive will extend to any frame of time after we have died. If a person absolutely refuses to let go of their unforgiveness, and this sin will not be allowed in heaven, then where is that person going to go with his unforgiveness when he dies?

The forgiveness of sins that Christ purchased for us by His death on the cross wiped out all the sins of our past, but it does not cleanse and make acceptable the sins that we continue to renew and embrace day after day. The sin of unforgiveness does not just sit in a little bottle in your soul somewhere waiting for God to open its cap and take it from you. The sin of unforgiveness is evil, and it is ever accessible by the evil one who wants to ruin your life and your relationship with God. Sin never sits dormant in a soul; it grows and evolves into other thoughts, actions, and attitudes in the human.

If the sin of unforgiveness could be bottled up until it was handed over to God with no action on the part of the human soul that created and formed it, then we could just expect a divine erasing of any wrong act on our part at any time. We could go on to do whatever we wanted to, expecting God's grace to wash all of the consequences of daily sins away. Why seek to become like Christ if you don't have to, when such seeking can be painful and restrictive to the "free will" which is opposed to all restriction.

We read in the book of Hebrews 10:23, 26-27 (NIV):

> *"Let us hold unswervingly to the hope we profess, for he who promised is faithful.... If we deliberately keep on sinning after we have received the knowledge of*

*the truth, no sacrifice for sins is left, but only a fearful
expectation of judgment and of raging fire that will
consume the enemies of God."*

How can we get away from what Mark 11:25-26 (NAS) tells
us that Christ said:

> *"And whenever you stand praying, forgive, if you have
> anything against anyone; so that your Father also who
> is in heaven may forgive you your transgressions. But
> if you do not forgive, neither will your Father who is
> in heaven forgive your transgressions."*

There is no promise here of God overlooking our unforgiveness
towards others, letting us slide by His Word with our
presumptuous sins day after day!

Question: Romans 11:29-31 (NIV) says, *"God's gifts and
his CALL are IRREVOCABLE. Just as you who were at
one time disobedient to God have now received mercy as a
result of their disobedience, so they too have now become
disobedient in order that they too may now receive mercy
as a result of God's mercy to you."* Either Christ's work on
the cross was enough or it wasn't. Either He saves us or
He doesn't. If you say that one sin, such as unforgiveness,
can cancel Christ's payment for our sins, not only are you
questioning God's power, but it follows that all sins can
be grounds for erasing our salvation! If a person willfully
REFUSES to forgive or willfully sins in any number of
ways without respect for God or concern for others, and
this person does not exhibit at least some of the fruits of the
spirit, then he/she is probably NOT saved. But please don't
confuse that kind of person with one who is still maturing
in Christ and desiring forgiveness but struggling with it,
saying that he/she is going to hell. I think you just need to
make this distinction clear to your readers!

Answer: If you can forgive like Jesus Christ, then the proof of your faith in the power of His forgiveness is clear. If His forgiveness of your sins is not strong enough to empower you to forgive others, then where is your testimony? The strongest testimony of the power of what Jesus Christ did for us lies in what it makes possible in our lives—the ability to forgive as He did.

I think where you're misreading me might be in your returning to being forgiven for the sins of your past. I absolutely agree that is a "done deal." What I'm talking about is the human deception of expecting daily forgiveness from Christ while continuing on in your own soul's unforgiveness. That is so close to being an unpardonable sin, it's hard to not see it. Your argument is not with me, it is with Christ himself.

Who's Going to Pay?

One deep-seated belief in the world today is that someone has to pay for negative circumstances in life. How often we've heard, "Somebody's going to pay for this!" Yet making someone pay rarely erases deep hurt and pain. In most cases, no repayment is capable of truly making things right. We must not try to settle these scores for ourselves, for this is the responsibility of the Father. Romans 12:17-19 (KJV):

> *"Recompense to no man evil for evil. Provide things honest in the sight of all men. If it be possible, as much as lieth in you, live peaceably with all men. Dearly beloved, avenge not yourselves, but rather give place unto wrath; for it is written, Vengeance is mine; I will repay, saith the Lord."*

Does this mean that recompense of damage is never godly? I received an interesting question about that from a man who was leading a Bible study in his home.

> **Question:** At our home cell group, we were reading and discussing pages 116-117 in SYS about the cost of forgiveness. You said, "When you forgive, you release the one who is guilty and place yourself in their stead … When you forgive, you are the one (who needs to be willing) to bear the loss instead of the one who caused the wrong. Jesus gave His life to prevent the loss of our lives." There was no example of what you were stressing. If we are to "bear the loss" instead of the one who caused the problem, are you saying we shouldn't look to collect for damages to car, person, or otherwise when hit by another automobile (for example). The other person still has to abide by man's laws, which hold him accountable for the damages. Could you address this point with a good example of what you are stating? Russell - Texas

Answer: I'm always glad to try to restate anything that I did not make clear in one of my books. The point I wanted to make on pages 116-117 of SYS was this: As far as you and me being the ones who have to "pay" the cost when we forgive someone for what they have done—*this is the attitude we must adopt and act from.* We must be willing to be the ones who bear the loss if the other person will not make it right—and we must do it with a pure heart that has forgiven them completely. I was not trying to say that we cannot accept any restitution from the other person, only that our attitude must be one of a willingness to let the loss go and "pay the cost" ourselves if the other party doesn't recompense us.

All responsible drivers have automobile insurance today. Insurance to some is a way of being protected against loss. To others it is a way of being able to be responsible for damages that exceed their ability to pay. You can forgive others for what they have done and still be in the right attitude when applying for reasonable insurance restitution. This is why all drivers are required (at least in my state) to have insurance—so they can be responsible to someone they have injured or for property they have damaged.

BUT, if you were to go to court and wipe out someone financially to recover damages (real or perceived) against yourself, I believe this is wrong. Receiving restitution in a right manner has to do with the attitude of the heart, which has forgiven the deed. I hope this helps.

What Forgiveness Is Not

Webster's Dictionary defines forgiving as ceasing to feel resentment against an offender. What Webster left out is that forgiving is not just the cessation of feeling resentment and a turning over to a higher authority for justice. Forgiveness must be a conscious act of the will to deliberately pardon another individual, period. It doesn't matter whether your feelings have ceased or not and whether God intends to judge the offender or not.

What about peaceful co-existence, a slipping into neutral with the other person, and ignoring him or her? This is not forgiveness. You may convince yourself that you have forgiven this person and simply don't feel the same desire for fellowship with them.

Perhaps you have tried to forgive again and again, and you just haven't been able to. Jesus said we need to forgive seventy times seven—that is at least four-hundred and ninety times. If you willed yourself to forgive someone every week, it would take you nearly nine-and-a-half years before you could take your case to Jesus as having obeyed.

What if the other person never comes and asks for forgiveness? There are no loopholes such as having to forgive only when the other person admits what they have done and asks forgiveness. The responsibility for your obedience to forgive lies on you.

You can repent of your sins until you are hoarse, confess your faith to all, pray without ceasing, give everything you have to the work of God, read the Bible every day, and still block God's forgiveness for your sins by your own unforgiving heart. No amount of repenting, confessing, praying, or reading the Word will ever cover over, atone for, or excuse unforgiveness! There is <u>nothing</u> you can do that can take the place of forgiveness:

- Forgiveness is not tolerance of the offender.
- Forgiveness is not pretending something didn't happen.
- Forgiveness is not forgetting what happened.
- Forgiveness is not generosity of spirit.
- Forgiveness is not turning the other cheek.
- Forgiveness is not looking the other way.
- Forgiveness is not making a joke of a wrong.
- Forgiveness is not politeness or tactfulness.
- Forgiveness is not diplomacy.
- Forgiveness is not a passive non-response to the offender.

- Forgiveness is something much deeper.
- Forgiveness is a deliberate act of the will.
- Forgiveness is a full pardon extended to the offender.
- Forgiveness cancels any resentment for all times.

- Forgiveness is a substitutional act.
- Forgiveness is obedience to God's Word.
- Forgiveness is an act of love.
- Forgiveness is the key to your freedom.

Forgiving and being forgiven are so closely intertwined, they simply cannot be separated. Perhaps you feel you can live without the forgiveness of other humans, but you cannot live without the forgiveness of God. God will not forgive an unforgiving heart that refuses to change! If you have been forgiven, you are capable of forgiving. If you have a problem believing Jesus really has forgiven you, then you may have a problem forgiving others. You need to loose all deception from your soul that is in opposition to His Word. Ephesians 3:16-20 (TM) tells us that Paul prayed this for the Ephesian believers, and for all believers after them:

"I ask him to strengthen you by his Spirit—not a brute strength but a glorious inner strength—that Christ will live in you as you open the door and invite him in. And I ask him that with both feet planted firmly on love, you'll be able to take in with all Christians the extravagant dimensions of Christ's love. Reach out and experience the breadth! Test its length! Plumb the depths! Rise to the heights! Live full lives, full in the fullness of God. God can do anything, you know—far more than you could ever imagine or guess or request in your wildest dreams! He does it not by pushing us around but by working within us, his Spirit deeply and gently within us."

Those who have known little or no forgiveness and grace while growing up will inevitably erect strongholds around their wounds and unmet needs. These strongholds can effectively block out any recognition or understanding of God's grace, love, and forgiveness flowing to this person. If this is you, you will may bitterly defend your right to not forgive. The Keys of the Kingdom prayer principles can get you out of that dungeon and into great freedom.

How important is it to you to do what Jesus is asking you to do?

Avoiding the Tormentors

In the parable of the two debts in Matthew 18:23-35, the debt the king forgave was enormous compared to a small debt owed by another to the man who had just been forgiven. Yet, that forgiven man went right out and demanded a poor servant instantly repay a tiny debt to him. The man had been forgiven of so much by the king, yet he refused to extend forgiveness for a servant's small debt to him.

This unforgiveness cost the man dearly. He lost the forgiveness of the king and was sentenced to jail to be turned over to the tormentors. The implications of this parable are very clear. As believers, we have been forgiven an enormous debt by the King. We can lose this forgiveness by unforgiveness on our part and be turned over to the will of the tormentors. These tormentors are evil spirits who have a right to begin to destroy your life. The original Greek word and its associated words that mean "tormentor" translate as:

- Inquisitor
- Torturer
- One who brings pain, toil, torment
- One who harasses and distresses
- One who tosses and vexes with grievous pains of body or mind

When a believer refuses to forgive another person, the believer is turned over to the will of these tormenting spirits. Bitterness and resentment in your soul are like weeds and thistles that suck the life out of your mental processes, your thought life, your will, your motivation, and even your determination to live. Roots of bitterness cause torment in your soul, causing it to set up strongholds which the enemy then accesses to torment you further.

Remember what the writer of Hebrews says in 6:7-8 (NIV):

> *"Land that drinks in the rain often falling on it and that produces a crop useful to those for whom it is farmed receives the blessing of God. But land that produces thorns and thistles is worthless and is in danger of being cursed. In the end it will be burned."*

The same writer also tells the Hebrew Christians (Hebrews 12:15, NIV) that they are in danger of losing out with God because of sliding back into their former ways and cautions them to:

> *"See to it that no one misses the grace of God and that no bitter root grows up to cause trouble and defile many."*

The Cost of Forgiveness

Real forgiveness is not cheap. It carries a very high price tag. The saying that "someone has to pay" really is true. When you forgive, you are the one who must be ready to bear the loss instead of the one who caused the wrong. Jesus gave His life to prevent the loss of our lives because we had all done wrong in God's eyes. Jesus was so serious about forgiveness, He gave His all for us before we even cared. You must be forgiven to be a part of Christ's bride—you must be forgiven to have no spots and no wrinkles in your bridal wear.

You must and you can forgive! If old memories of a hurt return to attack you, loose wrong patterns of thinking, beliefs, and ideas again—and then forgive again. Loose the power and the effects of word curses created by your own words and those of others. Bind your emotions to the healing balance of the Holy Spirit. Bind yourself to the truth of the Word that says God will work in you to help you.

Society has made a multi-billion dollar business out the belief that someone has to pay for everything that can be construed as a wrong against them. This has become so ridiculous that people are suing fast food places for the emotional anguish and mental suffering of their obesity. What if Jesus demanded reimbursement for physical pain and stress suffered during the crucifixion? Could any of us find attorneys who could help us fight against those charges?

The debt we owed God was beyond anyone's ability to pay it except God himself. So the almighty, omnipotent, omniscient, omnipresent God of eternity, in the incarnate Christ, substituted himself for us and paid off our debt by shedding His own blood on that cross. The most precious forgiveness to exist came at the highest price ever paid in the universe. And it came to you and me before we ever had the sense to ask for it or the standing to deserve it.

The world says, "You're entitled to your hurts and anger and your reactions! Look at what happened to you. We understand. Let us help you get even."

God says, "You can't hold onto those things, child. I cannot allow these sins to be covered over; you must destroy them before they help Satan destroy you. Let me show you how to make room to receive my mercy and grace. Let me show you how to forgive. Submit your will to mine and I will give you a new will. Submit your mind to the washing of my Word and the mind of my Son, and I will give you a renewed mind. Submit your emotions to the healing balance of my Holy Spirit, and He will refresh them." This is God's way.

It only takes two or three to work out the torments of unforgiveness in your life—God, you, and sometimes the other person. Sometimes it is worked out between you and the one who has offended you. Sometimes it is worked out between you and God alone. But you must loose every rationalization and justification that would stand in the way of receiving His work in your heart/soul to help you forgive. Pray this prayer and let God help you forgive:

> **I bind myself to the truth of the Word that tells me how much forgiving meant to you, Jesus. That makes it important to me, too. Please forgive me now for all the grudges I have secretly embraced—I choose to loose them. I loose every wrong attitude I have ever had towards those I have felt embarrassed, humiliated, betrayed, or ridiculed me. I will not seek to comfort my soul's outrage by asking you to hold anyone accountable. Father God, I am so grateful that Christ did not ask you to hold me accountable for all of my wrong actions before I knew you! You have commanded me to forgive so I can walk out of my pain and stop living under the fallout of it. I choose to forgive and cut myself free. Whether or not I forgive will not affect how you will deal with anyone else; it will only affect how you will deal with me. Please extend your grace and mercy to those who have hurt me, intentionally or accidentally, Father. This great gift from you is more than enough, many times over, to enable me to forgive others their petty offenses against me. In Jesus' name, Amen.**

Summary

1. True forgiveness means you give up any claim or resentment you have against another person for an offense they have committed.
2. When you forgive, you are the one who must be ready to bear the loss instead of the one who caused the wrong.
3. Forgiving is definitely an eternal matter that must be settled here on earth.
4. True forgiveness means that you will give up all desire to get even, and you will completely annul and make void whatever has been done to you, said to you, or taken from you.
5. When God asks you to do something that you are convinced you cannot do, know that He never asks you to do anything that is impossible for you to do.
6. The issue of your forgiveness of another person has nothing to do with their spiritual state—but it has everything to do with yours!
7. The creatures called Offense, Unforgiveness, and Resentment all conspire to lead you away from God and from your destiny purposes as a child of the King of Kings.
8. If your character is being proven by difficult experiences, then use the experiences to grow and to give God glory.
9. Faith is not given so you can avoid the hard times; it is given to get you through the hard times.
10. Every time you come out on the right end of an offense or a trial, full of faith and forgiveness, you become more like fine gold.

11. No amount of repenting, confessing, praying, or reading the Word will ever cover over, atone for, or excuse unforgiveness!

12. If you have been forgiven, you are capable of forgiving.

Chapter 7

Addiction, Deception, and Denial

Matthew 18:18-20

Matthew records the words of binding and loosing in a slightly different context in chapter eighteen (KJV):

> *"Verily I say unto you, Whatsoever ye shall bind on earth shall be bound in heaven; and whatsoever ye shall loose on earth shall be loosed in heaven. Again I say unto you, That if two of you shall agree on earth as touching any thing that they shall ask, it shall be done for them of my Father which is in heaven. For where two or three are gathered together in my name, there am I in the midst of them."*

Some use this passage only in the context of church discipline and membership rights because of the preceding verses 15-17. However, verses 18-20 cannot be restricted to this sole interpretation. These three verses offer valuable insight to the believer who prays in right agreement with other believers. There is tremendous power in agreement, which has been established by God.

When group prayers of right agreement are combined with the keys of binding and loosing, the results are dynamic!

The powers of darkness always respond to prayers prayed out of soulish agendas. Soulish agendas can range from seeking support for personal desires that have nothing to do with God's will to agreeing with others on how to destroy someone's reputation. Wrong agreements that appear to offer a mutual benefit to those who are involved almost always turn into soul ties. Witchcraft is also an example of prayers and incantations that come of out wrong agreements.

> God always responds to prayers offered from hearts united in His purposes and motives.

I have held weekly intercessory prayer meetings in my home and my offices since 1988. I am convinced that this weekly "soaking" in right prayers that always agrees with God's will has greatly contributed to my receiving new revelation from God. In these weekly prayer meetings, we bind people to God's will and His truth, loosing wrong attitudes, wrong patterns of thinking, and stronghold thinking from them. We have seen impossible situations begin to come into alignment with God's promises as we have done this. God says in His Word that if we do our part here, He'll do His part in heaven. His part includes working out all the details in everyone's lives.

Praying this way keeps us from praying wrong prayers for others and ourselves. Many people pray wrong prayers without realizing it. Wrong prayers can simply be ineffective, but wrong prayers can also set wrong things into motion. A simple example of this is for a parent to seek prayer agreement that Johnny will get the entry level management job he has interviewed for with the Handy Dandy Corporation. In the natural, this may seem like a right prayer because Handy Dandy Corporation has a great benefits package and pays good wages.

But what if God has plans for Johnny to be in ministry, or to get more education, or to become a world famous writer? The enemy would probably be quite aware if God had

> How many people would Johnny influence while working at Handy Dandy, compared to those he could influence in the ministry or as a famous writer?

marked Johnny for a broader scope of Kingdom influence than a position in this corporation would afford him. The enemy would also be quite capable of influencing corporate recruiters to put out very interesting carrots in front of Johnny's nose if he returned for a second interview.

This is not to say that it's wrong to be in management at the Handy Dandy Corporation. God needs His influential people there, too. But no one other than God knows if Johnny's destiny is to be one of those particular people. This is why it would be much wiser to pray with Johnny's parents that God's will would be done in his life—binding Johnny to His will and loosing all wrong counsel, works of the enemy, and personal agendas from him.

Johnny might be the very one for Handy Dandy's management staff, and such right prayers of agreement will help clear his way to get there if that's where God wants him. Only God knows for sure.

We've all heard people say with regard to problems in their church that they are praying (often in agreement with others) for certain people in church leadership to either do what's right or that God will remove them from their positions. This is not right praying. This is a form of trying to tell God what options are acceptable in the handling of this situation.

It would be better to pray and bind all of the people in the church leadership to God's will, plans, and purposes for their lives. Then pray and bind their minds to the mind of Christ while loosing any wrong beliefs or soulish agendas that might be in their souls. Finally, ask God to pour out grace and guidance upon those He currently has placed in leadership in this church so that His will can be accomplished. That puts the details, results, and outcome back in God's hands.

Right prayer is the most effective godly influence we can have on leaders, whether they are in the church, in government, or in other areas of authority. Never forget that God's Word says that Paul wrote this about leadership in 1 Timothy 2:1-3 (NKJV):

> *"Therefore I exhort first of all that supplications, prayers, intercessions, and giving of thanks be made for all men, for kings and all who are in authority, that we may lead a quiet and peaceable life in all godliness and reverence. For this is good and acceptable in the sight of God our Savior."*

Sarah

In the original *Shattering Your Strongholds*, I wrote of a young woman called Sarah who had anorexia, bulimia, and obsessive-compulsive behaviors. I want to give an update of Sarah's story as we have received so many questions since 1992 about her. I believe Sarah's story is an important testimony for the power of using the keys of binding and loosing in right agreement for someone with addictive behaviors and denial—trusting God with the outcome of those prayers.

Sarah had been molested repeatedly as a child and had been raped at the age of twenty-one. She became anorexic in her early teens, which progressed into bulimia combined with obsessive-compulsive behavior disorders. Sarah had attended a Christian day school as a child, but as a teenager, she began to experiment with drugs and alcohol, the occult, and wrong relationships.

Because of unmet needs and strongholds in her own life, Sarah's mother fiercely protected and enabled Sarah's ongoing choices of wrong behaviors. Sarah, on the other hand, manipulated her mother through her intense needs. They had serious soul ties with each other because of their wrong agreements (read more about soul ties in *Breaking The Power* and *Producing the Promise*). The two of them were praying prayers of wrong agreement with no comprehension that they were in complete denial of the danger of her behaviors.

> By the end of 1989, Sarah and her mother were becoming increasingly frightened by the circumstances overtaking Sarah's health.

Denial is a powerful form of stronghold thinking that can immobilize people, paralyzing their ability to help themselves or others. The denial I'm speaking of here is not just a simple act of denying the committing of a wrong act or the indulgence in wrong behaviors. Denial has the power to kill when it ignores the impending consequences of such wrong choices.

Sarah's mother and I began praying prayers of right agreement early in 1990 using the understanding I had of Matthew 16:19 and 18:18 at the time. Daily we bound Sarah to the will of God, the mind of Christ, the work of the cross, and the truth. We loosed from Sarah the works of the devil, wrong attitudes and patterns of thinking, wrong behavioral patterns, and any stronghold thinking that was protecting them. We loosed deception, denial, and her wrong desire to die. Within three weeks, Sarah ceased denying her anorexia and bulimia and her deep spiritual problems, confessing her need for help.

I believed that Sarah had never really asked Jesus Christ to be her Lord and Master, and I worked to get her to consider that she might not be born again. Another minister and I went through the salvation plan with Sarah, having her pray after us. She declared Jesus Christ, the Son of the most high God, to be her Lord and Master. The issue was settled!

After that time, Sarah seemed to have more peace and to be trying to overcome her dangerous eating habits. She seemed to want to get well. However, her body had undergone such ongoing devastation for so many years from her anorexia and bulimia, she did finally give up. She just wanted to be with the Lord. She stopped eating again and within months, Sarah passed away of a heart attack shortly after *Shattering Your Strongholds* was published.

Some might wonder where was the victory in Sarah's life. I believe the victory was that she settled her salvation with Jesus, and we now know that's where she is—in heaven with Him. God's healing power does not always produce the outcome that we hope for, but we can rest assured that He always works out the best possible results in His children's lives that they will allow Him to work out. Sarah might have never made it home to Jesus without the right prayers of right agreement that we prayed for her and with her.

Since writing of Sarah's story in *Shattering Your Strongholds*, we have heard several testimonies of women who have overcome anorexia through the binding and loosing prayers coupled with others forms of right agreement. I was privileged to meet with one young woman at one of my meetings in another state who was well on her way to recovery from this insidious disease. She said she believed that the prayers gave her keys that she needed to strip away the deceptions and wrong patterns of thinking from her soul. In another state, a *Shattering Your Strongholds* study grouped prayed for and ministered to another young woman with anorexia until she became healed.

Here is a prayer for people struggling with this disease. This prayer is written to be prayed by the person with the struggle, but you can insert someone else's name in place of the personal pronoun for praying it for others:

> I confess that I need your supernatural help, God. I need your strength and your grace to stop the cycle of craziness that I can't overcome on my own. I bind my body, soul, and spirit to you. I bind my mind, will, and emotions to you, trusting you to heal me. I obligate myself totally to you because I know you love me and will not fail me. I know I need to break my wrong patterns of thinking so that I can walk out all the good things you have in store for me. I now loose, smash, crush, and destroy all wrong patterns of thinking lodged in my soul. I loose all addictive thinking, all thoughts of denial, all of the deception my soul has bought into, and all self-destructive thought cycles that my soul keeps trying to run on me. I choose you, Jesus, and I choose your resurrection life. I bind my mind to your mind, and I ask that you will help me to immediately pray whenever my old thought patterns begin to recycle themselves so that I can loose them. I choose to be free. I choose to be well. Thank you, Jesus, for your help. Amen.

Addictive Thinking Leads to Addictive Behaviors

We have had many testimonials about how these prayer principles have given hope to men and women in prisons, jails, and recovery houses. We frequently receive letters from men and women in these settings who have heard the teaching of the Keys of the Kingdom or have the books. They have all expressed belief and relief that they finally had something powerful to use when their minds went into an addictive thinking mode. When addictive thinking is not restrained in some manner, it will almost always manifest addictive behaviors.

> Victory comes when you choose to immediately shut down your addictive thinking every time it tries to recycle itself.

When old, addictive patterns of thinking begin to start up, the real battle lies in making the choice to bind your mind to the mind of Christ while loosing old wrong patterns of thinking. This is the point where the victory can come the fastest, shutting down the addictive thinking the minute it begins to recycle itself.

Through personal experience with my own wrong patterns of thinking (involving some serious anger issues as well as using food to chemically soothe my soul), I learned that my soul knew me very, very well. That's a bit of a laugh, actually, because my soul is a composite of all of my thinking, feeling, and willfulness—there is nothing about the natural me that my soul hasn't "been there—done that."

One of my favorite passages regarding prayer is in the *King James Version* of Matthew 6:7-10:

"But when ye pray, use not vain repetitions, as the heathen do: for they think that they shall be heard for their much speaking. Be not ye therefore like unto them: for your Father knoweth what things ye have need of, before ye ask him. After this manner therefore pray ye: Our Father which art in heaven, Hallowed be thy name. Thy kingdom come. Thy will be done in earth, as it is in heaven."

This passage tells us how not to pray, and then it tells us how to pray. It says first that we are not to pray vain, repetitious prayers. Many have focused on the word repetitious in this verse, which is in error. The key word here is "vain" which means foolish and manipulative. We are not to pray foolish, manipulative, and worthless prayers to begin with, and we are certainly not to pray them over and over.

David said in Psalms 55:17 that in the evening, morning, and at noon he would pray and that God would hear his voice. You know he didn't have a completely new and unique prayer to pray each time he called out to the Lord. David died at the age of seventy (2 Samuel 5:4). If we assumed that David began his serious praying at the age of ten, that would mean he had 21,900 times of prayer. I'm sure David prayed the same right things many times.

We're just not supposed to pray wrong things over and over. I'll bet its fine with God when we repeatedly declare in our prayers that His will should be and shall be done on earth.

Right Prayer Repetition Can Break Addictive Thinking

Do not be discouraged if binding your will to God's will and loosing wrong patterns of thinking don't stop your addictive thought patterns the first or even the second time you pray these prayers. Many times, I had to pray these prayers at least three times in a very brief span of time before my soul would give up and submit to them. My soul knows how long I always tried to push through opposition and then gave up in the past. The number three has been a proven number for me when I am praying about something really stubborn.

We should loose wrong patterns of thinking as many times as it takes to see them going and gone!

> This measure of faith is like a pilot light in your soul.

In speaking of our souls as knowing us well, one could almost begin to wonder if our souls have split personalities. Not really, but they do have more than one agenda going at all times. We were born with spirits and souls that had no communication with the Spirit of God. However, God saw to it that at least a small, perhaps even tiny, part of our souls was capable of responding with faith to His love. In Romans 12:3 (KJV), we read that God has given every man a measure of faith.

Something had to be in your soul for it to respond to Jesus Christ. This is not anything the unsurrendered soul would want to do on its own. It has always fought to maintain control over the choices and decisions of your life. But there was a tiny pilot light of faith in your soul that believed what you heard about Jesus Christ in spite of all the strongholds and walls and deceptions that tried to get in its way. It appears to me that the Word is saying that this same measure of faith, regardless of how small it may be, has been given to everyone.

That is very encouraging to me as I pray for people who seem to hate the name of Jesus. I can believe that there is a tiny pilot light of faith within the most ungodly soul that just needs to be uncovered and blown upon to encourage it to leap into flame. Loosing wrong patterns of thinking and deception, along with loosing preconceived ideas and misconceptions about God, has to help uncover that pilot light!

Your human spirit was a spiritual orphan with no link to its Father's Spirit. It became connected to the Spirit of its Creator by the new birth through the sacrificial death of Jesus Christ. It now has full access to the Living Word, himself, as well as complete confidence and trust in the Father.

Faith—trust and confidence in the goodness, power, and wisdom of God—has to be developed in your soul. The mind and the emotions have to begin to get comfortable with trusting God. The will then needs to learn to relax and let God provide the power and wisdom to guide the soul's choices.

Addictive Behaviors and Soulish Symptoms Are Not the Problem

The word "addiction" means a persistent compulsive use of a substance or a behavior known by the user to be harmful, but it is something that the person cannot stop doing. When we are attempting to overcome such wrong behaviors, we have had a tendency to try to get rid of wrong thinking and acting only until they no longer seem to be problems in our lives. This is the "out-of-sight/out-of-mind"

> The difference between victory and defeat in our prayers often is that we don't finish the work.

mentality. Your soul is more than willing to appear to have backed off of its favorite old patterns of addictive thinking if it causes you to think you have them under control.

As you then congratulate yourself on your victory, your soul is already at work with another retooled cycle of the same wrong thinking.

The end result of the addictive thinking—addictive behaviors of drug abuse, alcohol abuse, food abuse, sexual sin, etc.—is not the problem that needs to be addressed. These behaviors are only the symptoms of the real problem.

The problem is an unsurrendered soul that believes it must fix its own pain, meet its own needs, and answer its own unresolved issues in any way possible—even if it takes a destructive behavior to accomplish this goal. Authority figures and well-meaning family members struggle with trying to help solve the symptoms that a person is exhibiting rather than seeking God's help with the sources that are driving the addictive behaviors.

> I kindly tell some parents no, I won't pray what they asked.

When I have had parents come to me and ask if I will pray that Bobby won't want to do drugs anymore or that Susie won't want to keep getting into sexual relationships with men, I kindly say no, I won't pray that. Then I tell them that I will pray in agreement with them that the source of the reasons why Bobby is doing drugs and Susie is sleeping around will be revealed. We bind Bobby's and Susie's wills to God's will; we bind Bobby's and Susie's minds to the mind of Christ; and we bind Bobby's and Susie's raggedy emotions to the healing balance of the Holy Spirit.

Then we loose, smash, crush, and destroy wrong patterns of thinking, word curses, the effects and influences of wrong agreements, deception, and denial from Bobby's and Susie's souls.

It is often taught that the wrong behaviors manifested out of addictive patterns of thinking are the results of evil spirits being in the person. This might have some element of truth in lives of unbelievers—but not believers. Christians cannot have evil spirits in their bodies; their bodies are temples of the Most High God. God does not cohabitate with evil spirits. However, spirits can certainly harass and badger a Christian who has open doors in his soul, causing his soul to begin to think frantically about what can bring some relief from its distress.

Wrong types of thinking present in Christians' unsurrendered souls come from the sources of all wrong thinking: unhealed hurts, unmet needs, and unresolved issues. Loosing addictive patterns of thinking begins the process of getting free. The final part of getting free and staying free is to begin to sow right patterns of thinking into your soul once you have cleared the wrong thinking out.

> The soul's addictive patterns of thinking are attempts to bring some sort of relief to itself from the drives issuing up out of its sources.

This prevents wrong patterns of thinking from returning—just like planting ground cover in a freshly weeded flowerbed. This prevents the weeds from returning as they surely would if the flowerbed was left empty.

What are some of the addictive patterns of wrong thinking that need to be loosed from unsurrendered souls? Here are some of the main ones:

- Angry thoughts
- Fearful thoughts
- Doubtful thoughts
- Worry
- Needy thoughts

- Deceptive thoughts
- Negative thoughts
- Chemical dependency thought patterns (including food)
- Sexually stimulating thoughts

There may be other addictive types of thought patterns such as gambling, but these are the main addictive patterns of thinking. You do not need to loose each one of these addictive thought patterns individually unless the Lord highlights them for your focus. The wonderful thing about these prayers is that you can loose wrong thought patterns, wrong beliefs, wrong ideas, etc., without having to identify them specifically.

If there are other addictive patterns of thinking you should be loosing by name, they will begin to surface as you pray and loose all wrong thought patterns.

Anger is not a spirit. Nowhere in the Bible can we read about a "spirit of anger." Anger is a powerful emotion that God has given to you which helps you be bold and courageous. This emotion helps you to push through opposition to fulfill difficult assignments. Anger should only be used for godly purposes, but unfortunately, it is one of the first emotions to rise up in the soul when people or situations cause reactions from your unmet needs or unhealed hurts.

A soul that is fully surrendered to God will channel this emotion in correct ways. An unsurrendered soul filled with stronghold thinking protecting unmet needs and unhealed hurts will use anger to protect itself or to get back at someone.

When angry thoughts are allowed to cycle through your mind again and again, they become addictive. You cannot bind yourself to peace and calmness, but you can loose angry thoughts and stop the recycling. As you make room to receive from God, peace and calmness will come from your communion with Him, from reading the Word, and from receiving His love.

Fear is not a spirit. The Bible tells us in 2 Timothy 1:7 (NKJV):

*"God has not given us a **spirit of fear**, but of power and of love and of a sound mind."*

In *Thayer's Greek/English Lexicon of the New Testament* the word "spirit" (Greek: pneuma) as used in this verse means to be filled with the same spirit as Christ and by the bond of that spirit to be intimately united to Christ. This Scripture is telling us that we, as believers, have no room in our spirits for fear because they are filled with the Spirit of Christ. Fear is the opposite of faith. It is a powerfully negative emotion rising up in the soul that has no trust or confidence in the goodness, power, love, and wisdom of God.

The Bible also says in 1 John 4:18 (NIV):

"There is no fear in love. But perfect love drives out fear, because fear has to do with punishment. The one who fears is not made perfect in love."

When God's love has found room in your heart/soul and is being perfected by the Holy Spirit, it drives all fear out. Perfect love is incompatible with self-punishing fear. Perfect love harbors no suspicion and no dread of God as a judge. The one who still fears and dreads God has not allowed Him to perfect and complete His love in him.

When fearful thoughts are allowed to cycle through your mind without any restraint, they can become addictive. You cannot bind yourself to courage and confidence in God, but you can loose fearful thoughts from your soul. As you make room in your soul to trust Him and you begin to experience acts of His love towards you, courage and trust begin to bloom out of your communion with Him, from reading His Word, and from receiving His love.

So, how do you practice being brave? You take a step towards doing something for God that you have never tried to do before. Speak to a stranger today about how much your relationship to Jesus means to you. Buy a sandwich and give it to a homeless person. Ask strangers who are obviously distressed or in pain if they would let you pray for them.

Doubt is not a spirit. To doubt something or someone means you lack confidence in that thing or that person. Doubt is like a cousin to fear without fear's torment of expecting punishment. Fear is an aggressive onslaught against your peace. Doubt is the absence of believing that God is always good and just and faithful to His children. "Doubt" in the original Greek manuscripts meant to be without a way, embarrassed, perplexed, at a loss.

> To doubt is to have no belief in knowing your way.

To "believe" means to think something is true, to be persuaded of its truth, and to place confidence in its existence. You generally know something exists and seems to be true because you have some sort of proof of it. Belief accepts that something exists and is true even if there is no tangible proof.

When doubtful thoughts are allowed to cycle through your mind without restraint, they can become addictive. You cannot bind yourself to believing, but you can loose doubtful thoughts that are hindering your ability to believe. God made you with a capacity to believe in Him. If you struggle to do so, then there is doubt and disbelief in your soul. As you loose doubt and disbelief and begin practicing believing in God, assurance will come as you spend time in communion with Him, reading the Word, and receiving His love.

So how do you practice believing in God? Do what David said he did in Psalms 77:11-15 (TM):

> *"Once again I'll go over what GOD has done, lay out on the table the ancient wonders; I'll ponder all the things you've accomplished, and give a long, loving look at your acts. O God! Your way is holy! No god is great like God! You're the God who makes things happen."*

Worry is not a spirit. To worry means to feel uneasy and concerned, to be troubled, to feel anxious and distressed, and to have a persistent mental uneasiness. It means to feel disturbed by the consequences of something unpleasant that has already happened or the fear that something is going to go wrong in the future.

The word "worry" is similar to the Old High German word for strangle and the Lithuanian word meaning to constrict. Another meaning for the word worry implies an incessant goading or attacking that drives one to desperation. These explanations are very closely related to the feelings that accompany addictive thought patterns of worrying.

Once you begin to worry about something, it is hard to pull yourself back to believing that God can take care of it. The best time to stop worry is within the first three seconds that it raises its nasty little head.

Neediness is not a spirit. If you struggle with being needy, you do not have a needy spirit. If you are a believer, your born-again spirit is just fine, thank you very much! It is connected to the Spirit of its Creator, to the Living Word himself, and to the Comforter. It is your soul that has unmet needs.

A true need is a lack of something good that is essential to your well being—a condition marked by the lack of something necessary. You cannot loose a need because it is the absence of something. If your refrigerator had an absence of food in it, the only thing that would rectify that situation would be to put some food into it. You could not fill it by loosing its emptiness.

> A true need must be met by God or a God-appointed person.

True needs are different from your soul's wants. Wants can be temporarily satisfied with things, with other people, and with passing pleasures. Too often, the soul's wants are thought to be genuine needs, which can cause the person believing they have a genuine unmet need to be very unhappy with God. Sometimes God does give us our wants, but many times, He doesn't when they have nothing to do with our purposes in life.

When someone has deep unmet needs, this lack may consume their thoughts. Once the soul begins to worry over what is lacking instead of what it has, it begins to obsess on those thoughts.

Becoming obsessed with your needs can cause you to think about them over and over until you become addicted to those thought patterns. You cannot bind yourself to being fulfilled and having your needs met, but you can loose addictive thought patterns that focus only upon your lack, your emptiness, and your unmet need. You can bind yourself to God's will and ask Him to meet your needs. Then you can begin to practice believing that He is going to do just that. Assurance that He is will come as you spend time in communion with Him, reading the Word, and receiving His love.

The words "believe in" mean to be in accordance with something. It also means an acceptance by the mind of something that is underpinned by an emotional or spiritual sense of certainty. So how do you practice believing that God is going to meet your needs? First, ask God to show you what your wants are and what the real needs are in your soul. Loose your thoughts about your wants and then begin to make a list of what God has already done for you through Jesus Christ.

Then make a list of the promises in the Bible of what God says He is presently doing for you whether you can see proof of them or not.

Know that you do not have to work at or accomplish something for God to meet your needs, nor do you have to sacrifice something. God is a giver, and He wants to give you what you need. Romans 4:14-16 (TM) tell us this about God's gifts to us:

> *"If those who get what God gives them only get it by doing everything they are told to do and filling out all the right forms properly signed, that eliminates personal trust completely and turns the promise into an ironclad contract! That's not a holy promise; that's a business deal. A contract drawn up by a hard-nosed lawyer and with plenty of fine print only makes sure that you will never be able to collect. But if there is*

no contract in the first place, simply a promise—and God's promise at that—you can't break it. This is why the fulfillment of God's promise depends entirely on trusting God and his way, and then simply embracing him and what he does. God's promise arrives as pure gift."

Deception is not a spirit. While deception might seem to be just the absence of truth, it usually is a distortion of some truth. Sometimes the deception that you have believed has been caused by someone else's calculated attempt to deceive you in the emotional, moral, or spiritual realm. Deception is the practice of someone who wants to deliberately mislead and misinform.

Other deception might come from your misconceptions about things that have happened to you.

Deception can be very subtle, such as the belief that you are not as important as other people—or it can be very bold such as the logic and reasoning that drives spiritual abuse or cultic control. How did the deception that is being protected by strongholds get into your unsurrendered soul? Some of it may have been from misguided attempts by your family to pass their personal beliefs on to you as you were growing up.

Soulish people may deceive you in order to manipulate you for personal reasons, causing you to learn of things incorrectly. The devil also tries to manipulate things in and around your life so that you perceive them erroneously. Once your soul has locked in on something as being true, it will go to great lengths to protect that belief.

You cannot know all truth by just binding yourself to truth. Knowing truth is a process of learning what lines up with the Word of God, and then acting upon what you have learned by faith (unseen) so that it becomes an actual experience (seen) in your life.

Believers have the Word of God to guide them in knowing what is truth and what is deception. When some situations are very difficult to unravel as to whether or not there is deception involved, our gifts of the Spirit include three important spiritual gifts that can help us. First Corinthians 12:7-10 (NKJV) tells us this about the gifts of the Spirit:

> *"The manifestation of the Spirit is given to each one for the profit of all: for to one is given the word of wisdom through the Spirit, to another the word of knowledge through the same Spirit, to another faith by the same Spirit, to another gifts of healings by the same Spirit, to another the working of miracles, to another prophecy, to another discerning of spirits, to another different kinds of tongues, to another the interpretation of tongues."*

Of the nine gifts of the Spirit, the gift of the word of wisdom, the gift of the word of knowledge, and the gift of the discerning of spirits are all gifts that can reveal deception. When in operation, this gift of the discerning of spirits reveals whether or not an ambiguous manifestation of power is of a human soul, a demonic spirit, or the Holy Spirit.

Not all manifestations of power are discernible by the natural senses. Both soulish people and demonic spirits can be quite cunning. The Holy Spirit may be manifesting a work that is in direct opposition to what your soul is wanting to happen, so it begins to declare that deception is at work. The discerning of spirits is vital to understanding where God is at work in some unclear situations, and it works best in the believer who is in the process of surrendering his soul to God.

Bind yourself to God's will, and bind yourself to His truth, which will function as a plumb line for you to measure everything else against. Then loose all deception and denial from your soul. Loose all stronghold thinking that would protect and hide deception and error, and ask God to show you what else might be in your soul that would prevent the gifts of the Spirit from operating in your life. Spend time in prayer and communion with Him, reading the Word, and receiving His love.

Negativity is not a spirit. Negativity is an attitude that causes addictive negative thinking patterns. A negative person rarely sees anything positive in himself, in others, or in his situations. This person seems to see only the gloomy side of life, viewing everything through dark emotional glasses. Negativity describes people or attitudes that are unenthusiastic, defeatist, or pessimistic.

Negativity also spawns attitudes that are contrary, antagonistic, uncooperative, and cynical. I once had a negative friend who never commented on anything positive about my clothes or even my preaching. One time when I had preached my heart out and felt that the Lord had helped me deliver a good message, my friend rushed up to me immediately afterwards and said, "Don't ever wear that dress again when you preach. Every time you raised your hands, your slip showed and it was very embarrassing."

Negativity has a way of so focusing on one small downbeat thing that it completely misses everything else that is right. This is an attitude that can become deeply entrenched in an unsurrendered soul, cycling through everything the person does and thinks. Negativity is very addictive because every negative word or thought sows more seeds of negativity. It becomes like a self-seeding prophecy. You cannot bind yourself to being positive, but you can loose negative thought patterns from your soul. The success of this prayer is always based upon recognizing when negative thoughts arise.

When we have negative beliefs or disappointing expectations about ourselves, they affect how we think and act around other people. These negative beliefs can also affect how others act towards us.

We communicate our self-beliefs with various cues, such as acting confused, or behaving timidly or aggressively. People tend to respond to these cues by adjusting their behavior to correspond with what we think about ourselves. The result is that our negative thoughts seem to be true because of how people react to us—reinforcing the wrong belief that started the whole cycle.

Be aware of attempts of the enemy to cause others to make you feel rejected or to be offended. Refuse to allow your emotional reaction to others' actions to lead you into these negative attitudes. If your emotional reactions do begin to get out control, then bind your mind, will, and emotions to God's will and loose wrong reactions and wrong attitudes from your soul. If your mind begins to recycle wrong thought patterns again, loose them again. You can break this unhealthy cycle, but you may have to persist in order to do it.

When you refuse to feed feelings of rejection or offense, they will often pass with no lasting results. If you personalize what others say to you and allow your soul to identify them as negative attacks, your hurt feelings can have long-term consequences.

Chemical dependency is not a spirit. Many in the church today have given names to the various behaviors of those who rely upon chemical substances to alter their moods: spirit of alcohol, spirit of marijuana, spirit of cocaine, spirit of gluttony, and more. Chemical dependency cannot be cast out of a person like an evil spirit out of a non-believer; chemical dependency is a self-protective and self-comforting coping mechanism of the unsurrendered soul.

You cannot have your soul cast out of you.

An unfortunate aspect of chemical dependency is that addictive thinking about the relief and the elevated moods this behavior can bring quickly turns into wrong mind/body agreements. The mind becomes psychologically addicted to the relief and the chemical pleasure rushes and so does the body. This creates a twofold cord of addictive thinking and physical craving.

Drugs and alcohol temporarily make the world go away when pressure and fear are more than a person thinks he or she can bear. Prolonged use of drugs and alcohol create life's dropouts and alcoholics.

Having grown up with a maintenance drinker who was my father, I learned that nothing remained constant in our family. What was funny to my father yesterday could be cause for punishment today. What seemed to please him today could become cause for verbal abuse tomorrow.

The scientific studies about depression and addictive behaviors have shown that these people are often endorphin deficient. Endorphins are called the "feel good" hormones of the body, and they are produced by exercise (the runner's high), creative activity (painting, playing music, etc.), laughter, sexual activity, and prayer.

Endorphin levels are likely the difference between happy, self-entertaining children and unhappy, bored children. The child who is always happy and laughing stimulates his own endorphin mechanism, releasing these feel-good hormones into his body. The unhappy child having a very low endorphin level does not engage in activities that release even what he does have.

God has obviously placed these endorphins (the name means "morphine within") in our bodies. In the 1970s, a Jewish scientist discovered that our brains had opiate receptors in them. He concluded that a God who would build opiate receptors in our brains would obviously also put opiates in our bodies for them to receive. This was one of the early beginnings of the studies of endorphins.

Because we know what causes endorphin rushes in our bodies, we can engage in physical exercise, watch funny old movies, and participate in creative activities to give ourselves an endorphin boost. It is a wonderful thing that although our soul's toxic waste can tear down our immune system, endorphins strengthen it. Even though we may have brought varying degrees of destruction upon our bodies, God has designed them to able to repair themselves.

The one problem with this "morphine within" is the same problem with everything good that God creates: the devil creates counterfeits of the same thing. The opiate receptors in our brains do not know whether an opiate (mood altering chemical substance) that it receives is natural or artificial—they embrace them equally. When someone has no natural tendency or interest in acting in a manner that produces a rush of endorphins, in times of great pain and stress they are tempted to use counterfeit opiates—alcohol, drugs, or food—to subdue and pacify their pain and anxiety.

Constantly thinking about the relief produced by these three chemical sources can become addictive—an addictive form of thinking that ultimately produces more addictive behaviors. The one chemical producing substance that I liked very much was food. I did not realize at the time that food turned into chemicals that affected my body chemistry; this is why eating seemed to make me feel better.

> I learned that food can make you feel better, can elevate your moods, and can pacify your soul. And food was legal!

Plus, there was no worry of being stopped for driving under the influence of food after the potluck dinner was over.

Too much stress—get the cookies and the ice cream. Nerves all rattled—cook up the mashed potatoes. Carbohydrates are always good for a calming effect; caffeine helps to rev up your body; and chocolate just plain makes you feel good. That about covers everything.

Even after I became a Christian, I found that while there was no temptation of drugs, alcohol, or sex in the church—it was filled with opportunities to eat. We married people with food at the reception and we buried people with food after the funeral. Refreshments were always a critical part of prayer meetings, and the potluck lunches and dinners were a delight! Unfortunately, the aftereffects of food as the chemical substance of choice was increasing weight gain.

I remember that my father would send me to bed without supper when I was between seven and ten years old. My mother would always sneak into the bedroom later and give me cookies, saying, "Here, this will make you feel better." I had no problem then or later believing that this was true. That was the beginning of my lifelong love of food, but the ongoing struggle I still have today is not my mother's fault. The fault is mine now, but it is one that I am slowly winning.

We are responsible for choosing to either reject or embrace wrong patterns of thinking still in place in our lives long after we first learned them. Addictive thinking in your thirties, forties, and fifties is not your parents' fault—all bad habits learned while you were growing up become your responsibility as soon as you begin to make your own choices about your life.

Breaking away from the format here, this is a prayer to help you begin to take down the strongholds protecting your addictive thinking:

Lord, I don't want to try to compensate for my own feelings or to try to fix my pain any more, I want to turn them over to you. I want to become stable and fixed under your shadow as it says in Psalms 91 (AMP)—I want to trust and rely upon you totally to help me overcome my dependency upon chemical substances. I bind myself to you—body, soul, and spirit. Help break my body's addiction to these substances. Help heal my soul's dependency upon these substances. Help me listen to the encouragement and guidance you speak through my born-again spirit. I loose, smash, crush, and destroy all of the wrong patterns of thinking, the rationalizations, and the justifications for what I've been doing to my body. I loose all wrong mind/body agreements that my soul has initiated. I do not want my soul influencing my body to come into wrong agreements in order to subdue its pain. I want to turn to you when I'm in pain; I want to receive your mercy and grace. I believe you will help me to overcome this struggle and I thank you for that, Lord. Amen.

Sexual thoughts are not a spirit. Promiscuous sexual activity and self-induced sexual activity are another result of a wrong mind/body agreement. The mind begins to think about sexual activity and communicates its mental arousal to the body, which begins to feel physical arousal. The soul's attempts to appease its needs through sexual activity are first psychological, but they become physiological. Any time your soul finds a way to comfort itself and temporarily relieve its own pain is an act that exalts itself between you and your knowledge of what God can and wants to do for you

Even married sex that is primarily used to appease the soul's distress and pain is not a good reason for marital relations.

The mind is where the sexual thought patterns begin. The enemy is often the originator of those thoughts because of the people, pictures, or words that he causes to be played out in your presence. He is very canny about picking up on your body cues once he has tried to set you up. He understands a quickened heartbeat, a flushing of the face, and an immediate interest in what he has set up.

Then he can pressure these addictive thought patterns with customized temptations to act them out. Sexual thought patterns that are not surrendered to God become addictive.

The soul will also initiate sexual thoughts and desires if it has learned to comfort and pacify its own neediness this way. You can loose wrong patterns of sexual thinking, but the success of praying this way is based upon praying them as soon as you are aware of these thoughts and before you are tempted to act upon them.

> Jesus, I thank you for giving me the Keys of the Kingdom so that I can stop the addictive wrong thinking that my mind pleasures itself with. I bind my mind to your mind, Jesus. I need your thoughts to help stabilize and steady my mind. I loose, smash, crush, and destroy all wrong patterns of thinking that go through my head when I want to turn to any kind of sexual activity that helps distract my soul from its distress. I will—I will continue to loose these thoughts until they cease. I will begin to think of things above, like Scripture says I should. I will not leave my mind unoccupied to start this cycle of wrong thinking again. Your Word says that I should set my mind on things above, not on earthly things. Your Word says that I should meditate on whatever things are noble, just, pure, lovely, of good report, things of virtue, and things that are praiseworthy. I will. I will do this so that my mind learns to meditate on godly things. I will not leave my mind pondering the things of the earth that my soul keeps trying to comfort itself with. Thank you, Lord, for helping me to do this. Amen.

Summary

1. The powers of darkness always respond to prayers prayed out of soulish agendas.
2. Wrong prayers can simply be ineffective, but wrong prayers can also set wrong things into motion.
3. Do not be discouraged if binding your will to God's will and loosing wrong patterns of thinking don't stop your addictive thought patterns the first or even the second time you pray these prayers.
4. There was a tiny pilot light of faith in your soul that believed what you heard about Jesus Christ in spite

of all the strongholds and walls and deceptions that tried to get in its way.

5. Faith—trust and confidence in the goodness, power, and wisdom of God—has to be developed in your soul. The mind and the emotions have to begin to get comfortable with trusting God.

6. Your soul is more than willing to appear to have backed off of its favorite old patterns of addictive thinking if it causes you to think you have them under control.

7. Authority figures and well-meaning family members struggle with trying to help solve the symptoms that a person is exhibiting rather than seeking God's help with the sources that are driving the addictive behaviors.

8. The final part of getting free and staying free is that you have to begin to sow right patterns of thinking into your soul once you have cleared the wrong thinking out.

9. Anger should only be used for godly purposes, but unfortunately, it is one of the first emotions to rise up in the soul when people or situations cause reactions from your unmet needs or unhealed hurts.

10. A true need is a lack of something good that is essential to your well being—a condition marked by the lack of something necessary. You cannot loose a need because it is the absence of something.

11. When in operation, the spiritual gift of the discerning of spirits reveals whether or not an ambiguous manifestation of power is of a human soul, a demonic spirit, or the Holy Spirit.

12. It is a wonderful thing that although our soul's toxic waste can tear down our immune system, endorphins strengthen it.

Chapter 8

Influencing Your Family

Family Fruit

When Jesus spoke to His closest "family" members on earth, the first disciples, He said this in John 13:34-35 (TM):

> *"Let me give you a new command: Love one another. In the same way I loved you, you love one another. This is how everyone will recognize that you are my disciples—when they see the love you have for each other."*

The word "disciple" means one who professes to have learned certain principles from another and maintains those principles in their own lives based upon that other's authority. This word is applied principally to the followers of Jesus. If you are maintaining the principles of Christ in your life, then you are a disciple of His. He wants you to always remember that the world will only know who you are—one of His believers—because of the love you show your brothers and sisters in the faith and in your own family.

The modern family needs a lot of help. Families today are constantly being attacked by divorce, movement about the country and even the world, and a myriad of political and

> Today's family barely gets together for dinner because they are all going different directions.

social groups pursuing their own perceived personal rights, which fall outside God's definition of family. Families do not live their lives out together these days because they are so divided in their self-perceived destinies and self-pursuits. In the early days of the Bible, families had to stick together in order to protect their very lives and their flocks and herds.

Today's family breadwinners may also find themselves in troubled industries, meaning that they must look elsewhere for employment. To follow the work, some fathers can be separated from their families for months or years—possibly abandoning them forever. A very common cause of divorce is the abandonment of family by its male head, sometimes even the mother. Add in all of the political and social attempts to redefine the family, and it is a wonder that the beleaguered families of the world are holding together at all.

I certainly can't advise you on how to have the perfect family. I've made as many mistakes with my family as the next person, probably more. No one but God really knows what to do every time to ensure perfect family relationships and growth. But consider the following quote (in part) from the original *Shattering Your Strongholds*. If it still works and it's not broken, I say go ahead and use it!

The Keys of the Kingdom binding and loosing principles can dissolve most, perhaps all, of the *effects* of the mistakes you made as a parent. Many parents became Christians after they have raised their children without godly counsel and understanding. Some became Christians halfway through the parenting process, making awful mistakes as they tried to shift from reverse into overdrive without letting the Holy Spirit work the clutch. I stripped several gears in raising my own children, both before and after my Christian rebirth.

What parents haven't been heartbroken to see their sons and daughters paying the price of their parents' mistakes? What grandparents have not been grieved to see their children repeating their mistakes while raising their grandchildren? You cannot go back and erase these mistakes any more than you can erase the mistakes made by the adults in your childhood. But just as you can dissolve from your soul the negative, ongoing *effects* of the mistakes others made in your early life, you can dissolve the *effects* of the mistakes impacting your children's souls and grandchildren's souls today.

Acknowledge the mistakes you made, renounce them, and repent of them one LAST time; then ask and receive forgiveness for them. The Lord is willing to forgive, and He genuinely wants you to get past your guilt over them to begin cooperating with Him in straightening out the tangled effects still impacting everyone today. There is a very strong chance that you can't fix any of these problems or straighten out any of the negative effects by yourself, anyway. So, work with Him.

We first need to get ourselves in a position to realize that our only source of permanent help comes from Jesus Christ. Apostle Paul said that he certainly had no idea of what to do with himself in Romans 7:18-24 (TM):

> *"I realize that I don't have what it takes. I can will it, but I can't do it. I decide to do good, but I don't really do it; I decide not to do bad, but then I do it anyway. My decisions, such as they are, don't result in actions. Something has gone wrong deep within me and gets the better of me every time. It happens so*

regularly that it's predictable. The moment I decide to do good, sin is there to trip me up. I truly delight in God's commands, but it's pretty obvious that not all of me joins in that delight. Parts of me covertly rebel, and just when I least expect it, they take charge. I've tried everything and nothing helps. I'm at the end of my rope. Is there no one who can do anything for me? Isn't that the real question?"

That's the real question, Paul! It is our question, too, nearly 2,000 years later. Paul then goes on to say this in verse 25:

"The answer, thank God, is that Jesus Christ can and does. He acted to set things right in this life of contradictions where I want to serve God with all my heart and mind, but am pulled by the influence of sin to do something totally different."

You and I can try everything that every Internet site, book, group, and article says about the family. We can try to follow the suggestions of every organization dedicated to the family.

> Paul says the answer is Jesus Christ—not at the edge, not on the weekends, not occasionally—all the time!

These things surely won't hurt. But when your spouse is straying, your child is dabbling with drugs, or your parent is drinking too much—you can't tie them up with research and professional suggestions, try to fix them yourself, and then declare that everything has to be all right because the experts and authorities said so.

Jesus is the answer to the big picture and the little picture. He left us the Keys of the Kingdom to unlock the answers to every rebel pixel of the big picture that overwhelms you. *[Pixel: small dots that make up bigger images on movie or computer screens.]* Jesus Christ left the Keys of the Kingdom for us to use to cause things on earth to come into alignment with God's already established will in heaven. He did that so that you had a divine answer for what to do when you couldn't solve a natural problem.

How can we best help our families and family members in today's world? Keys of the Kingdom prayer is the best and foremost answer to coming into agreement with God for our family members. Bind their wills to the will of God, bind their minds to the mind of Christ, and bind their raggedy emotions to the healing balance of the Holy Spirit. Loose, smash, crush, and destroy wrong patterns of thinking and wrong beliefs out of their souls so they can receive His truth.

Bind backsliders to the truth of God and the understanding they once embraced and then crush and destroy the distortions the god of this world keeps torching them with. Pull them out of his fire and bind them back to their heavenly Father, wrapping them up in love and in truth just like you would a wounded soldier. Fight for them behind their backs in the spirit world.

Bind your loved one's feet to paths of righteousness. Bind their hands to the work that God has always ordained them to do in these last days. Loose (crush, smash, shatter, disrupt, dissolve, and destroy) the lies and deceptions the enemy has told them. Rip apart and tear at the wrong attitudes and stronghold thinking in their minds. Loose, shatter into minute fragments, and lacerate the evil imaginations the enemy has set up in their minds.

You can powerfully impact someone else's old nature, but you cannot change it—that is a choice they must make. With prayers of loosing, however, you can undercut the strongholds in their old natures and shatter the enemy's deceptions. When you do this, you give your loved ones every advantage and assistance possible so that they will be able to hear Jesus call them; then they can see Him and either choose to embrace or reject Him.

Keep loosing grave clothes from them. Wrong attitudes, wrong patterns of thinking, wrong ideas, and wrong beliefs are internal fruit, bad fruit, which grows within a person's unsurrendered soul. These internal attributes are not grave clothes. Grave clothes are hung on an individual externally by other people. This is a basic list of grave clothes:

1. Word curses
2. Rumors
3. Accusations
4. Gossip
5. Slander
6. Lies
7. Finger pointing
8. Insults
9. Slurs
10. Character assassination

The words of others can drape grave clothes on your loved ones just like the funeral wrappings put upon the corpses in the early Jewish burial preparations. Begin to loose these things (either calling them grave clothes or call them by separate names if you feel better) from your loved ones.

When Jesus finished praying to His Father as He stood before the open tomb of Lazarus, He began the first step towards doing a miracle. He called Lazarus out, placing a choice before him: Would he respond to Jesus calling him back into life or would he just stay in the tomb. John 11:43-44 (AMP) tells us this:

"When He had said this (speaking to His Father), He shouted with a loud voice, Lazarus, come out! And out walked the man who had been dead, his hands and feet wrapped in burial cloths (linen strips), and with a [burial] napkin bound around his face. Jesus said to them, Free him of the burial wrappings and let him go."

Jesus told Lazarus' loved ones who had put the funeral wrappings upon him to loose the grave clothes from him and set him free. After the people obeyed this command, they stepped back and

> Lazarus had to choose to respond to Jesus, but the people cleared his path so he could!

Lazarus walked fully forth into life. This is the most exciting encouragement I've ever had as a parent who made mistakes in my children's lives before I knew that Jesus could have made a difference in my parenting.

Not only could I loose grave clothes off my children that had been put there by others, I was being given a specific chance to cooperate with Jesus in the undoing of what I had done wrong. I was being given this incredible opportunity to work with Him as He began doing a miracle for my kids!

Our ministry to our families is not so that we change them for the better. When your family members are clinging tightly to their offenses and misconceptions, anything you do can be seen as attempts to compound their hurt and anger or to control them. But when family members begin to see how much God has changed you, they are faced with their own anger and unforgiveness as well as the truth of the renewed you.

> Our finest ministry to our families is when we change ourselves.

Ever since Adam and Eve blew it in the Garden of Eden, fathers and mothers have struggled with knowing how to raise their children the best way. In this past century, so many people have become parents themselves without ever having good parenting skills modeled for them. Regardless of what romantic notions exist about becoming a parent, lots of new fathers and mothers don't have a clue about how to be a good parent. We unfortunately learn so many wrong things, and even though we swear we will never treat our children like we were treated, we end up finding ourselves repeating the mistakes of our parents along with a few new things all of our own.

We have had wrong seeds sown into our lives that produced wrong fruit. That wrong fruit birthed seeds that we have sown into the lives of our children. The issue is not who sowed the wrong seeds first—that would mean we had to go all the way back to the Garden of Eden. The issue is that we can undo this wrong planting in our family's lives now! We have the keys to get it done.

Victory for a Father and Mother

I am an only child, a state of being that I've always felt has been much maligned. Someday I am going to print up a bumper sticker that says: "I'm an only child and I'm not spoiled! I just like things done my way!"

My parents were both born in the Great Depression and never really got over some of the effects of living through that time. My father had suffered from losing both of his parents before he was fifteen years old, and then living alone on the old family homestead for a year and a half. His older brothers and sisters all went and lived with other relatives after their parents died, leaving him on his own.

My mother was a middle child. Her older brother had all of the privileges of being the oldest, and her younger sister had all of the privileges of being the baby of the family. My mother once told me that one day she hid under her bed and cried herself to sleep. When her mother finally found her, she asked my mother what was wrong. My mother replied, "I just wish you loved me as much as you love my little sister and my big brother."

Her mother replied, "Well, I would if you acted as nice as they do." I could tell that this had been a profound pain to my mother all of her life. She was always very concerned that everything appeared to be perfect, that everything always looked right, that everyone acted nice even if they were furious at each other, and above all to make sure that no one would ever know that this façade wasn't true.

My four grandparents all had hurts and problems in their souls that were passed on to some degree to their children. My parents carried unhealed hurts, unresolved issues, and unmet needs in their souls, bringing them into their marriage and family relationships. This is a huge problem with hurts, issues, and needs—unless they are healed and met, they pass from generation to generation to generation. Hurting people create hurting people who create hurting people who create hurting people. It takes a miracle to stop this cycle!

No one in my family ever knew they could step up and say, "This is as far as these generational thought patterns and woundings go—this is as far as these unhealed hurts and unmet needs go. I will be the one who stops them with the help of Jesus Christ. I will be the one who stops this cycle through prayer." Instead, my father tried to soothe the pain in his unsurrendered soul with alcohol, and my mother tried to stop the driving neediness coming out of her soul with food and materialism.

> My mother never got over her fears of being without.

Because of the lack of affection and love along with the material lack during the Great Depression, my mother became the Great Hoarder. It didn't matter that what she was hoarding had no value to the world; it had value to her. When I cleaned out their house after they both passed away in 2003, all the cupboards in the garage were filled with pickle jars and mayonnaise jars. In the house, I think she had every cottage cheese carton, yogurt carton, and plastic fork and spoon that had passed through that house in the previous ten years.

Because of my father's background of growing up emotionally deprived and lacking in any affection or attention towards him, he cherished his relationship with my mother. She was someone who loved him unconditionally, someone he was sure would never leave him. When I was born, I suddenly took a lot of my mother's time and attention. I believe a great deal of my father's feelings towards me were mixed up with his sense of the loss of my mother's full attention and devotion.

> I overdid the whole Christian witness "thing" by making a big deal out of refusing to play poker with my dad anymore, to have a beer with him, or to laugh at his jokes.

When I became a Christian in 1972, I was a pretty over-zealous witness for Jesus. There is nothing wrong with avoiding any former behaviors that don't give a good witness, but I did it quite self-righteously. When I pressed my mother about whether or not she was saved, she said of course she was, so I thought she was a done deal with God. I didn't know that she was just trying to get me to back off because the idea of Jesus embarrassed her. Instead, I felt I needed to focus all of my salvation efforts on my father.

I gradually learned to be less "in your face" about Jesus, and true concerns for the state of my father's soul began to nag at me. Every so often, I would try to bring up Jesus to him and he always swear and cuss, saying the same thing, "Don't give me that, Jesus is just a figment of your imagination. God and I are old buddies, and I don't need this Jesus fellow of yours." I used to fear that lightning would come right down through the roof of the house and strike us all dead every time he said that—but it didn't.

I even tried visiting him in the hospital when he was about to have open-heart surgery (during one of the many times when he wasn't speaking to me). I took my pastor with me, believing that God was going to have my father ask me to forgive him and then he would finally tell me that he loved me. I imagined that heavenly music, angels, and rainbows of lights would fill the room. When I walked into the room, he looked at me and didn't say a word. After a long pause, I decided to "prime the pump," so I asked my father if he would forgive me for anything I had ever done to upset him. He looked at me for about twenty seconds and said, "No." That was the only word he said to me.

I remember almost staggering out the door of his room to fall against the wall in the hall. I was literally gasping for air, feeling as if I'd been gut punched. I began to cry as I begged God for understanding, "God, why did that happen? I prayed, I forgave him for everything he ever did to me, and I wanted to reconcile so badly. Why did this happen, God?"

The Lord simply said to me, "To whom much has been given, much will be required. You have everything; he has nothing."

These were not the comforting words I had hoped to hear, but there seemed to be some small kind of promise in them and that was all I had.

These exchanges went on for years, and then I began to pray the binding and loosing prayers for my father and my mother. My father suddenly stopped drinking after having drunk for nearly fifty-two years. He even became a little easier to get along with. I invited him over to my house one day to watch a San Francisco 49ers game. As Jerry Rice was making one of his spectacular touchdown runs after catching a precision Joe Montana pass, I began chanting softly, "Go, Jerry, go. Go, Jerry, go!"

My father turned and almost yelled at me, "I said I didn't want to hear any more about that Jesus fellow!"

I replied, "I wasn't saying anything about Jesus."

He growled at me, "Don't give me that. I know you were and I want you to stop it right now!" As I mulled that over, it occurred to me that even though I wasn't saying anything about Jesus, somebody was. I was delighted to think that the Holy Spirit was on the job even during a 49ers football game!

A few years later, I was in New Jersey about to make an unexpected trip into Manhattan to speak at the Bowery Mission. I called home to ask my mother to pray for me as all of my friends in Sacramento were working at the time. My father answered the phone instead and said my mother was out for the day. I thought for a moment and because I was almost out of time, I asked him to pray for me. After all, he had said he and God were great buddies. He said okay. I pushed the envelope a little and I said I needed him to pray right then. He said okay. I asked him to pray out loud, and he said okay!

I had waited over fifty years to hear what came out of my father's mouth in the next few seconds. He said: "God, take care of my daughter, because she's special and I love her."

Having never heard him say he loved me at any time during my whole life, I immediately burst into tears. I sobbed out, "Father, you made me cry!"

He said, "Yeah," and hung up. I knew that God was working in response to my prayers as I had been binding him to God's will every day, binding his mind to the mind of Christ, and binding his emotions to the Holy Spirit. I had loosed every possible misconception and deception in his soul that was standing between his knowing the truth about God's love, forgiveness, and healing. I kept loosing the lies that I believed he had accepted about Jesus, and I loosed the belief that God wouldn't forgive him. I also loosed the lie that God would leave him someday as his brothers and sisters had.

About a year later, my father became very ill, and we all thought he was going to die. I kept praying the binding and loosing prayers because that was all I could do in the situation, other than being there to sit with him. My father still had not accepted Jesus as his Savior, and he still didn't want to talk about Him.

I read about a man who lived on the edge of the desert, and then he disappeared out into the desert for a couple of days. When he came back, he declared he had become a born-again Christian.

There was an interesting story in my local newspaper about a man who had been an atheist all his life.

He built a little roadside shop in the desert and told everyone who stopped by about Jesus. I was so touched by that story that I thought that if Jesus could meet that man out in the desert One on one, the He could do it for my father, too.

The next day I went up to Redding (200 miles north of Sacramento) to visit my father in a skilled nursing home. He was not doing well at all, and I wanted so bad to shake him and say, "What's wrong with you! You might die any day and you don't know Jesus yet. What's wrong with you!" But I was afraid I'd throw him into cardiac arrest and cause his death. So, after visiting with him for awhile, I left his room to head out to the parking lot.

I heard that little voice in my head that sounds like God to me, and it was telling me to do something I've never done before. I turned around and marched back into my father's room. I went right up to him and shook my finger in his face, saying, "Has Jesus been in here to talk you today?"

He gruffly said, "No!"

I said, "Well, He's going to be!" and I turned around and marched back out into the hall. All the way to the parking lot I kept saying, "Oh, Lord, I hope that really was you. Oh, Lord, I hope that really was you!"

My father was a legend. He would free himself, climb over his hospital bed's bars, and take off down the hall. He was determined to go home!

Two days later, my mother called me. She said, "I have something I think you will want to know. Today I went into the nursing home and when I walked through the front door, the head nurse met me. She said that my husband was a legend at their hospital." My mom told me she apologized, saying she was really, really sorry for whatever he had done. My father really was a genuine, four-star character, and even though he had lost over sixty pounds and was very thin, he was their star escape artist. They simply could not restrain him in anything that he couldn't get out of—even a semi-straight jacket.

Then my mother told me that the nurse continued, "Mrs. Savercool, I went in and talked to your husband this morning. I asked him if he was a Catholic or a Protestant. He told me that was none of my business! So I told him that he was pretty sick and if he got worse, he'd better tell me now if he wanted us to call a priest or a pastor to come."

She said that he looked at her and loudly declared, "Look, I'm a born-again Christian. I believe in the Lord Jesus Christ, all right? Now get out of here!"

I laughed and I cried at the same time, cried because I felt such relief, and laughed because all I could think was, "Leave it to my father to make a belligerent statement of faith!"

He began to get better and was finally able to go home. He seemed to keep getting better and seemed less depressed; he was always ready for me to pray for him after that. In Jesus' name, even! About two years later, my father got very sick and he went into CICU in the hospital. My mother also went into the hospital the same week, into the ICU. Then they were both transferred to the same skilled nursing home. Within three weeks, my father passed away. I was so glad that I knew where he was going.

About two months before my mother passed away (six months after my father), she was always trying to figure out where my father was living since she had to be at the skilled

> My mother was quickly sliding into early dementia, complicated by high blood pressure, diabetes, and congestive heart failure.

nursing home. Her sister, a born-again Christian (Sarah's mother in an early chapter), kept trying to explain to her that my father had gone home to heaven. My aunt then asked my mom, "Would you like to accept Jesus as your Savior so you can go to heaven, too?"

My mom replied, "Well, I guess I'd better." My aunt led her through the sinner's prayer right then. After hearing this story, all I could do was thank the Lord for His faithfulness. It had been a long time coming, but that didn't mean a thing once they were both safely headed for heaven.

God is so good! Later when I began to worry a little bit if my father really had really gotten saved, I "suddenly" remembered the verse in Romans 10:9-10 (NIV):

> *"If you confess with your mouth, 'Jesus is Lord,' and believe in your heart that God raised him from the dead, you will be saved. For it is with your heart that you believe and are justified, and it is with your mouth that you confess and are saved."*

The Word has such power to put all your fears to rest! I didn't have to wonder about my father's salvation anymore. He had confessed with his own mouth that he believed in the Lord Jesus Christ. He was saved!

Praying for the Family of Mankind

There are far-reaching implications of the power of this way of praying. God tells us to pray for leaders and kings and even nations, such as the command to pray for the peace of Israel. In 1 Timothy 2:1-2 (NIV), the Apostle Paul said:

> *"I urge, then, first of all, that requests, prayers, intercession and thanksgiving be made for everyone— for kings and all those in authority, that we may live peaceful and quiet lives in all godliness and holiness."*

Bind those who are in authority to the will of God; then loose the wrong attitudes and patterns of thinking that have deceived world leaders and government officials for so long. If ever there was a need to strip away strongholds and the blindness and error they protect, it is from those who are making incredibly far-reaching decisions in these perilous last days. Bind the President of the United States, his advisors, the heads of other countries, the governor of your state, the supervisors of your county, and the leaders of your city to the will of God and to the truth. Bind their feet to paths of righteousness.

Loose wrong patterns of thinking, attitudes, beliefs, ideas, desires, habits, and behaviors from them. Loose the power and effects of the words of wrong counsel given to them. Loose the ideas of man from them, and loose tradition and generational bondages from them. Loose the power and effects of word curses spoken to them, about them, and by them. Whatsoever you loose on earth that is in accordance with God's already established will, will be loosed in heaven.

In Isaiah 27:3-5 (AMP), the Lord says:

> *"I, the Lord, am its (Israel's) keeper. I water it every moment; lest anyone harm it, I guard and keep it night and day. Wrath is not in Me. Would that the briers and thorns (the wicked internal foe) were lined up*

*against Me in battle! I would stride in against them,
I would burn them up together. Or else (if all Israel
would escape being burned up together there is but
one alternative), let them take hold of My strength
and make complete surrender to My protection, that
they may make peace with Me! Yes, let them make
peace with Me!"*

As you pray for Israel in whatever way the Holy Spirit would
lead you, bind her government leaders, her inhabitants, and
the Jewish people all over the world to the will of God for
their lives. Bind their feet to paths of righteousness, bind their
minds to the mind of Jesus Christ, and bind them to the work
of the cross. Loose the wrong patterns of thinking, attitudes,
beliefs, traditions and generational bondages, deceptions, and
wrong plans of men from them. Strip the clouds blinding their
minds that keep them from seeing the light of the gospel of
Jesus Christ, their Messiah.

Impact your home, impact your city, impact your state. Impact
your country and impact the world. For such a time as this,
you have been sown as good seed into the world. Bear fruit
everywhere you can.

Summary

1. If you are maintaining the principles of Christ in your
    life, then you are a disciple of His.
2. The Keys of the Kingdom binding and loosing
    principles can dissolve most, perhaps all, of the <u>effects</u>
    of the mistakes you made as a parent.
3. We first need to get ourselves in a position to realize
    that our only source of permanent help comes from
    Jesus Christ.

4. Jesus Christ left the Keys of the Kingdom for us to use to cause things on earth to come into alignment with God's already established will in heaven. He did that so that you had a divine answer for what to do when you couldn't solve a natural problem.
5. Keys of the Kingdom prayer is the best and foremost answer to coming into agreement with God for our family members.
6. You can powerfully impact someone else's old nature, but you cannot change their old natures—that is a choice they must make.
7. Grave clothes are hung on an individual externally by other people. Begin to loose these things (either calling them grave clothes or by separate names if you feel better) from your loved ones.
8. Our ministry to our families is not so that we change them for the better. Our finest ministry to them is to change ourselves.
9. The issue is not who sowed the wrong seeds first—that would mean we had to go all the way back to the Garden of Eden. The issue is that we can undo this wrong planting in our family's lives now!
10. God tells us to pray for leaders and kings and even nations, such as the command to pray for the peace of Israel.
11. For such a time as this, you have been sown as good seed into the world. Bear fruit everywhere you can.

Chapter 9

Get Ready to Influence the World

It's Not Satan, It's Us!

In Revelation 20:1-10 we read of the prophecy that states a time when Satan will finally be bound. He goes about like a roaring lion until that time, regardless of how many people have tried to use Matthew 16:19 to bind him. The final work of binding Satan is committed to an angel from heaven in the fullness of God's timing.

Many commentators believe that this angel is Jesus Christ with a chain and a key to bind Satan, imprison him, and keep him locked there until he is to be released 1,000 years later. Sadly, when he is released, he picks up right where he left off—going about deceiving the nations.

When men and women are finally given 1,000 years free from all of Satan's interferences, they should be able to finally get God right. Yet Revelation 20:7 says that when Satan is released at the end of the 1,000 years, he deceives the nations and gathers an army whose numbers will be like the

> Mankind has 1,000 devil-proof years to understand what God has been telling them without any satanic static, and millions still don't get it!

grains of sand on the seashore (Revelation 20:8) for yet another rebellion against God.

Satan is not the problem—he just profits from the problem through deception and fear. Mankind's own self-wills, unrenewed minds, and unhealed emotions are the problems that drive the rebellion against God.

God's Plans For Us Right Now

In speaking to the Roman Christians (Romans 11:32, TM) about the Jews who had temporarily lost out with God, Paul said this:

> *"In one way or another, God makes sure that we all experience what it means to be outside so that he can personally open the door and welcome us back in."*

This is a very interesting translation, but the truth is clear. We don't really appreciate what we have unless we have been without it. You don't really have an idea how well God is treating you unless you have been treated badly. You have no true appreciation of relationship unless you have been all alone or rejected. You take water for granted until you are stranded somewhere without any. When you have received these good things, the appreciation that you then express for God's goodness, for relationships, and for cool drinking water have the potential to bear good fruit in others.

The hard times you've experienced and the healings and answers that God has brought you give you a unique perspective on offering hope that He will do the same for others. The heat you have experienced in your life makes you more fruitful when you begin to influence others. The fruit that the olive tree bears is always the biggest and the best when the tree has undergone a long, hot summer.

We are all undergoing a learning process of being part of His plans. God knows what He is doing, and He is always working all things together for the good of everyone

> He is working out all things together for all of us corporately.

He has called. This doesn't mean that He is working things out for your good and for my good independently of each other. This is one of the reasons we don't always see our answers happening the way we expect them to—because our answers are only a small part of the pieces to a larger picture.

Our lives always affect other peoples' lives, just as other people's lives affect ours. When you are seeking the will of God to the best of your ability, His goodness, power, and love are always being worked in you, upon you, and through you out to the world. Paul exhorted believers to engage in good works so they would not be unfruitful.

Being Fruitful

The fruit of the Spirit as listed in the book of Galatians consists of "stuff" that is both something you **are** and something you **do**. Let's consider the fruit that you **are**, the fruit that defines your character, in these next paragraphs.

In Titus 3:8 and 14 (NKJV), we read this:

> *"This is a faithful saying, and these things I want you to affirm constantly, that those who have believed in God should be careful to maintain good works. These things are good and profitable to men ... And let our*

people also learn to maintain good works, to meet urgent needs, that they may not be unfruitful."

Peter also exhorted believers to add the qualities of Christian character to their faith lest they be unfruitful in 2 Peter 1:5-8 (NKJV).

"But also for this very reason, giving all diligence, add to your faith virtue, to virtue knowledge, to knowledge self-control, to self-control perseverance, to perseverance godliness, to godliness brotherly kindness, and to brotherly kindness love. For if these things are yours and abound, you will be neither barren nor unfruitful."

In Galatians 5:22-23, we read the list of the fruit of the Spirit. Paul wrote this list to highlight the fruit that Christ's church is to be exhibiting to the world:

1. Love
2. Joy
3. Peace
4. Patience
5. Kindness
6. Goodness
7. Faithfulness
8. Gentleness
9. Self-control

Then Paul says this at the end of verse 23:

"Against such there is no law."

No one in society, in the courts of justice, in the military, or in government could find anything subversive, illegal, or objectionable in this list of the fruit that all Christians should be exhibiting. Even an atheist would be hard put to condemn these qualities in a Christian. An atheist would find it easy, however, to condemn a Christian who acted the opposite of this list. Let's look at this "legal" fruit one by one.

LOVE is an easy fruit to document in the Bible, especially in the thirteenth chapter of 1 Corinthians, verses 4-7 (TM):

> *"Love never gives up. Love cares more for others than for self. Love doesn't want what it doesn't have. Love doesn't strut, doesn't have a swelled head, doesn't force itself on others, isn't always "me first," doesn't fly off the handle, doesn't keep score of the sins of others, doesn't revel when others grovel, takes pleasure in the flowering of truth, puts up with anything, trusts God always, always looks for the best, never looks back, but keeps going to the end."*

This is a perfect list of the ways that we should always act towards others. This is a list of ways to act that show us what to strive for so that we can be more like Jesus.

Love never gives up:
- Love always sticks through thick and thin with a friend
- Love never turns its back on a family member in need
- Love never stops reaching out to strangers in need just because it backfired the last time

Love cares more for others than for self:
- Love sits up all night in a hospital waiting room with a frightened parent
- Love gives surly teenagers a second chance
- Love gives away a favorite coat to a shivering stranger when it is snowing

223

Love doesn't want what it doesn't have:
- Love doesn't covet other peoples' blessings
- Love isn't greedy
- Love appreciates everything

Love doesn't strut, and doesn't have a swelled head:
- Love is never proud and haughty
- Love humbly accepts whatever comes its way
- Love is a good listener

Love isn't always "me first":
- Love thinks of the other person's needs before it worries about its own
- Love gives room to those who push in front of it—and it does it with a smile
- Love helps others to get ahead without concern for its own position

Love doesn't fly off the handle:
- Love is patient
- Love overlooks other people's faults and differences
- Love always counts to one hundred when someone is being difficult

Love doesn't keep score of the sins of others:
- Love doesn't make lists and keep books on other people's actions
- Love always overlooks or ignores other people's faults
- Love never refuses to forgive just because someone has done the same thing thirty times before

Love never revels when others grovel:
- Love never wants someone who doesn't make it to be uncomfortable
- Love never wants others to be embarrassed or humiliated

- Love never laughs at some who finally got "paid back"

Love takes pleasure in the flowering of the truth:
- Love is always pleased when someone is acquitted of an accusation
- Love is protective of the one who confesses a falsehood
- Love rejoices with those who stand up for what is right

Love puts up with anything:
- Love never stops being kind to someone who is mean and spiteful
- Love always acts with grace and mercy
- Love never reacts to another's bad attitude

Love trusts God always:
- Love prays for God's will to be done in others with great blessing
- Love knows that God's Word can always be trusted
- Love has trust and confidence in the goodness, wisdom, and power of God

Love always looks for the best:
- Love always looks for the good in people that God sees in them
- Love always believes for the potential that God is working out in others
- Love always knows that God is working in every situation in every life

Love never looks back, but keeps going to the end:
- Love never holds another's past actions against them
- Love tries to find something good in every person's actions
- Love will always walk hand in hand through hard times with others

> Joy is a state of mind, an orientation of the heart that is never affected by worldly things.

JOY is a fruit that sweetens everyone's life, a deep feeling of contentment and happiness inside. Things may be bad in your life, but true joy will continue to radiate out of the assurance that God is in control of your life and that He is good. Joy in your heart is precious, but joy is really completed when you are able to share it with someone else. Shared joy magnifies the sweetness of whatever you are feeling or experiencing. Joy is always contented and yet hopeful that God has only just begun!

When others speak of you, do they always remark that you are so full of joy? Set that as a goal for yourself, that others always describe you as the joyful one. Jesus spoke to His followers in John 15:10-11 (KJV), saying this:

> *"If ye keep my commandments, ye shall abide in my love; even as I have kept my Father's Commandments, and abide in his love. These things have I spoken unto you, that my joy might remain in you, and that your joy might be full."*

John said this about his joy in Third John 1:4 (KJV):

> *"I have no greater joy than to hear that my children walk in truth."*

Many of the New Testament's epistle writers referred to their joy as coming from seeing success, growth, and joy in others they had shared with. How many other lives have you invested in with the Gospel? Tend your investment by encouraging them and keep track of their progress. The payoff is more joy that you can invest in even more people. Joy is a most contagious fruit!

PEACE is a fruit that brings such comfort, yet sometimes seems to be elusive. This is a fruit that you cannot force, but it is a fruit that will quickly descend upon the soul that has been stripped of fearful thoughts, worry, and anxiety. Peace is a fruit that will not war with strife and contention, nor will it push its way past the existence of negative thinking. Peace is almost like the deer who picks her way daintily into the meadow when she feels that there is no danger. The Word of God says this about peace in Psalms 119:165 (NKJV):

> *"Great peace have those who love Your law, And nothing causes them to stumble."*

Isaiah 26:3 (AMP) tells us this about God:

> *"You will guard him and keep him in perfect and constant peace whose mind [both its inclination and its character] is stayed on You, because he commits himself to You, leans on You, and hopes confidently in You."*

Jesus said this about His peace in John 14:27 (AMP):

> *"Peace I leave with you; My [own] peace I now give and bequeath to you. Not as the world gives do I give to you. Do not let your hearts be troubled, neither let them be afraid. [Stop allowing yourselves to be agitated and disturbed; and do not permit yourselves to be fearful and intimidated and cowardly and unsettled.]"*

Fear, which most often travels with its first cousin, Anxiety, has always been the most common thief that steals our peace. Over and over again, Jesus asked, *"Why are you afraid?"* *"Why did you doubt?"* Over and over again, He said, *"Don't worry!"* *"Do not let your hearts be troubled!"* *"Do not be afraid!"* Help the fruit of peace find room to bloom in your own soul and character by creating space for it with prayer—loose all fear, doubt, and worry from your soul.

The New Testament Greek word most often translated as peace has the sense of meaning "to join that which had previously been separated or disturbed." It is frequently used to signify oneness, quietness, and rest. Peace is another contagious fruit, and other people will catch it from you. Go ahead and be a "carrier" out there infecting other peoples' troubled souls with peace!

PATIENCE is a fruit that usually blooms over a period of time. Patience is also known as longsuffering, sort of like "love on trial." I think of longsuffering as patience "x" ten, or patience on steroids. (I know that is a bit of an illogical statement, but it just fits!) Patience enables you to forbear and forgive others (Colossians 3:13). This fruit also means being doggedly persistent even though the going gets tougher and tougher.

In the Scriptures, the word patience is used in reference to people and not things or events. Barclay says, "Patience is the grace of the person who could revenge a wrong but does not. It's the long-suffering which endures injuries and evil deeds without being provoked to anger or revenge." Patience is the fruit usually needed most when the Christian feels least like acting like it.

To be humanly patient is one thing, but to be patient with great endurance is a truly divine fruit. Had God not been longsuffering towards me, I can only wonder where I would be now. Thank you, Lord. (Pass it on, reader!) In Ephesians 4:1-3 (KJV), Paul beseeched the Ephesians church to:

*"Walk worthy of the vocation wherewith ye are called, with all lowliness and meekness, with **longsuffering**, forbearing one another in love; endeavoring to keep the unity of the Spirit in the bond of peace."*

The fruit of patience is not only a fruit of the Spirit, it is also a redeeming social virtue that can help us think and act reasonably toward

> Patience is a lot less passive than we think, and a lot more aggressive in its purpose.

others during times of testings and trials. This particular fruit makes us think of waiting, twiddling our thumbs, and being passive. Patience does not need to be passive; it can be a strong, vibrant kind of waiting that is alert and ready to embrace God's next direction.

Jesus is a perfect example of patience under pressure. He was under intense pressure when the Sadducees and Pharisees harangued Him and baited Him, trying to get Him to lose His temper. None of us has ever come close to exhibiting patience like His or like God's. God's patience should always fill us with great gratitude. Patience, grace, mercy, loving kindness, goodness, and truth all allow God to work with people until they finally get it. If God struck out at people just as short-fused humans frequently do, no one would be alive today. Patience is also described at times as "being slow to anger."

The Greek word for "longsuffering" means patience, endurance, constancy, steadfastness, perseverance, forbearance, longsuffering, and slowness in avenging wrongs. Slow down, friend, and let the fruit of patience ripen in your life.

KINDNESS is a gracious fruit of the Spirit. The Greek word translated as "kind" or "kindness" means moral goodness with integrity. The spiritual fruit of kindness never has an ulterior motive or a hidden agenda and it always benefits others. Luke 6:35 (NAS) says to even:

> "*Love your enemies, and do good, and lend, expecting nothing in return: and your reward will be great, and you will be sons of the Most High; for He Himself is kind to ungrateful and evil (men).*"

In Ephesians 4:32 (KJV) Paul says:

> "*Be ye kind one to another, tenderhearted, forgiving one another, even as God for Christ's sake hath forgiven you.*"

Many of the people who seem to work at bugging us may never notice that we are exhibiting patient love towards them. However, patient love reveals itself in acts of kindness. Isn't it strange that kindness is such a rare quality these days that when someone is very kind, their name and their act of kindness have a good chance of not only getting in the paper, but might even make News at 11:00!

> A smile is a very cheap anti-virus program for frowns.

An interesting thing about the fruit of the Spirit is that this fruit doesn't cost us any money. Rich and poor alike can share this fruit with all, regardless of the size of their pocketbooks. Kindness might only take a sacrifice of time and energy, or the self-discipline of being thoughtful and acting upon your thoughtfulness. But a simple word of encouragement doesn't cost much at all in time or energy. The main effort is in remembering that Jesus Christ has placed these fruits in you through His Spirit, and He is always hoping you will put them out on display to show His love.

Kindness also is translated from a Greek word meaning "the sympathetic kindliness or sweetness of temper which puts others at their ease, and shrinks from causing any pain." This describes a quality that makes other people feel comfortable when they are with you because they know you will be kind or gentle. "The greatest thing a man can do for a Heavenly Father," said Henry Drummond, "is to be kind to some of His other children." Frederick William Faber commented, "Kindness has converted more sinners than zeal, eloquence, or learning." Kindness must be all over us if we are to have deep influence on our generation.

Always remember that spiritual fruit you are bearing is the outward expression of how much Christ has been allowed to bear His fruit in your soul. Be kind to someone today, someone who needs to see how kindness works.

GOODNESS is a good fruit, and that isn't really redundant— it is truth! Most references in the Bible regarding goodness speak of the goodness, kindness, gentleness, and patience of God towards us. The Greek word for "kindness" as it has been often used in the Book of Galatians means "virtue equipped at every point." That is good, too.

Today we use the word "good" to describe anything from a hot fudge sundae even to the character of a man who has just been arrested on a morals charge: "He always seemed like a good man." The scriptural concept of goodness is much deeper than

> To be truly "good," our overall motive for anything we do is that we love God and want His will in everything we are even remotely connected with.

just using it to describe something or someone in the world. This fruit of the Spirit reflects on every thought, word, and action of the one who is exhibiting it.

We should always treat others with goodness borne straight from the Seed of Christ's goodness bearing fruit both in us and through us. Acts of the true fruit of goodness always are joined together with an ongoing desire to do something to make sure the person is well and happy. This desire is never based upon the perceived value and worthiness of the recipient. Ephesians 2:10 (TM) says this about acts of goodness:

> "He creates each of us by Christ Jesus to join him in the work he does, the good work he has gotten ready for us to do, work we had better be doing."

Why is it that we do not see opportunities for showing goodness to others as often as we should? These opportunities are all around us every day. Ask God to give you sensitivity to them, so that you might show the fruit of goodness of God to others so they might know that God is for them and not against them.

FAITHFULNESS is the attribute of one in whom faith can be placed—one who is trustworthy, faithful, and who can be relied on. Faithfulness in the world today is usually a combination of what a man thinks to be important combined with his ability to make a commitment to it. Humans are faithful to sports, shared goals, friends, whatever they feel is important.

William Barclay writes that the word for faithfulness means "the characteristic of a man who is reliable." Bearing the fruit of faithfulness means that you will do what you say. Faithfulness means that you won't make promises unless you are as sure as you can be that you will be able to fulfill them. Today so many in the world and in the Church say that they will be available for this or that—going to a prayer meeting, helping

A major part of faithfulness is follow-through.

someone move, or contributing to a worthwhile cause—but they don't follow through. To be faithful means that you take your commitments very seriously. Are you the type of person that someone would speak of to another person in this way, "Don't worry, Danny will be here. He always keeps his word."

First Thessalonians 5:23-24 (AMP) tells us that Paul was so sure of his Lord that he boldly claimed the following promise for both the Thessalonian Christians and us:

> "And may the God of peace Himself sanctify you through and through [separate you from profane things, make you pure and wholly consecrated to God]; and may your spirit and soul and body be preserved sound and complete [and found] blameless at the coming of our Lord Jesus Christ (the Messiah). Faithful is He Who is calling you [to Himself] and utterly trustworthy, and He will also do it [fulfill His call by hallowing and keeping you]."

He who is faithful to us can be wholly relied upon. That makes it both safe for us and imperative of us that we be faithful in all that we set ourselves to do. Let us be faithful with the calling we have been given by Jesus Christ to go and bear fruit wherever He puts us.

GENTLENESS is a very dear, tender gift of the Spirit. It is the root of how we act toward others, whether or not we are humble and kind to them. This fruit of the Spirit can remove all fear and distrust from others. It is a gift that makes people feel cared for.

However, the fruit of gentleness isn't about being wishy-washy or wimpy. It is instead a choice to refuse to try to use power over anyone, and to build people up instead of scaring them half to death. There are gentle ways to be bold, to stand up for what is right, or to be used to motivate others into wanting to do what's right, but these are not the first choices of human nature by any means. We are only truly gentle when the fruit of the Spirit, gentleness, finds it way to the top of our souls like cream rising to the top of a bottle of milk.

The world often wants to use brute strength or soul power to dominate others when there is a dispute or disagreement. In God's Word, Proverbs 25:15 (TM), however, we read that God (as usual) has a very different way of advising us how to resolve dispute and disagreements:

> *"Patient persistence pierces through indifference; gentle speech breaks down rigid defenses."*

Several years ago, my ministry held our first LSM conference at a big hotel in Sacramento. We did everything by the "book" as we understood it. We prayed and we tried to represent God in the best way we knew how. Finally, everything was in place and we had a signed contract for the big, beautiful ballroom of this hotel. We continued to pray, binding ourselves, the hotel staff, and everyone who was supposed to come to the LSM Mentoring Messengers of the End Times conference to God's will.

A few days later, I received a rather urgent call from the salesperson who had finalized our arrangements and worked out the contract. She said that she had made a big mistake because the ballroom was booked on Saturday night for their Annual Halloween Ball, which they had been holding for eight years. We would have to move into a smaller, darker room for our final meeting, which was supposed to be very special. I was speechless (fortunately), so I just said I'd call her back.

I told my staff what had happened, but they weren't quite as vocally challenged. I had a signed contract that I could take to court and make them give us the ballroom, I could do this, I could do that, and so on, they said. In my earlier days as a Christian, I would have had no problem with walking this right to an attorney's office and pushing whatever buttons needed to be pushed to get us our ballroom. But the binding and loosing prayers had done their work, and somehow the fruit of gentleness managed to push its way to the forefront of my soul and I held steady.

I said, "We're a ministry built on right prayer, so let's pray some right prayers about this situation." So we began to pray and

"We don't know but what God wants us in that little room across the hall, and we just might have people in ghost and goblin and witch costumes coming in to get saved."

bound everyone at the hotel to the will of God; we bound every mind to the mind of Christ; and we bound their emotions to the healing balance of the Holy Spirit. We loosed personal agendas, the works of the enemy, and wrong beliefs off all the hotel staff. I told my staff that if we forced the hotel to give us the ballroom, we would probably not have the favor we needed with them.

Against every natural fiber of my being, I wrote a kind letter to the hotel telling them that while we would be very disappointed if we had to give up the ballroom (through no mistake of our own), we didn't want to cause them undue pressure and stress over their annual plans. I said that we would waive our signed contract if they asked us to, and we would move out of the ballroom and into the little dark room on the final night of our conference. We prayed long and hard over that letter before it was mailed, binding it to God's will and purposes.

The next afternoon the manager of the hotel called me and said that they didn't feel they could ask us to waive our contract and that the ballroom was ours. I thanked them profusely and we prayed long and hard to thank our God for His supernatural intervention and the favor He had prepared for us.

I am certain that God had just been waiting for Christians to come along who would show this hotel staff gentleness and kindness in their dealings, not pushing for their own way. I am so grateful that we didn't get all human and self-righteous and blow the honor of being the ones who finally did His will.

Another Greek meaning for "gentleness" describes it as an attitude of clemency filled with compassion, forgiveness, forbearance, lenience, and mercy. Second Timothy 2:24-26 (NAS) records Paul as saying this:

> "The Lord's bond-servant must not be quarrelsome, but be kind to all, able to teach, patient when wronged, with gentleness correcting those who are in opposition, if perhaps God may grant them repentance leading to the knowledge of the truth, and they may come to their senses (and escape) from the snare of the devil, having been held captive by him to do his will."

SELF-CONTROL/TEMPERANCE is the fruit of the Spirit that holds everything in balance, and keeps our humanness in check. Self-control actually means to be able to control one's "self," which is the soul. Second Peter 1:5-8 (KJV) tells us this:

"Giving all diligence, add to your faith virtue; and to virtue knowledge; and to knowledge temperance; and to temperance patience; and to patience godliness; and to godliness brotherly kindness; and to brotherly kindness charity. For if these things be in you, and abound, they make you that ye shall neither be barren nor unfruitful in the knowledge of our Lord Jesus Christ."

"Temperance" is translated here from the Greek word that means the virtue of one who masters his soulish desires, human passions, and sensual appetites. This virtuous person can be bold rather than being tentative, can be confident rather than being nervous, can be grateful and sure rather than being uncertain, and can rejoice rather than being timid or fearful. These matters of character are the stuff that gives Life to your life. The fruit of the Spirit speaks of who you are, not just what you do. It speaks of how you think and what you say.

Out of the Mind Speaks the Mouth

The mind is the part of the soul that is the most tempted to spew forth words that are not spiritual when it feels

> To take control over any part of your life, you must change our mind sets and your attitudes.

like it wants to kick over the fence. These words come from wrong thoughts that you have never challenged. Bind your mind to the mind of Christ and loose all wrong patterns of thinking, then loose all the works, especially deception, of the enemy. Too many people think if they just starting acting better, that right thoughts will automatically appear in their minds.

Too many changes that are being encouraged today are outward changes with no attempt to change the inward thoughts of the mind. These changes are almost always short-lived, such as quitting smoking, drinking, or going on a diet. Unchallenged old patterns of thinking always pull everything back into the same position they started in, regardless of how far you made it with your resolution. You challenge them by stripping wrong mind sets and attitudes from your soul with the loosing prayers.

Solomon said in Proverbs 4:23 (KJV):

> *"Keep thy heart with all diligence; for out of it are the issues of life."*

Jesus told His disciples in Matthew 15:18-20 (KJV) that:

> *"Those things which proceed out of the mouth come forth from the heart; and they defile the man. For out of the heart proceed evil thoughts, murders, adulteries, fornications, thefts, false witness, blasphemies: These are the things which defile a man."*

Christians are always "under construction" just like the up-to-date web sites are on the internet.

The Bible tell us in Matthew 12:34 that it is out of the content of your heart that your mouth will speak. The binding and loosing prayers help you to start housecleaning in your heart, which is your soul. As you do this, your mind and your mouth will follow.

Like everything else in the world today, the fruit of the Spirit may be rising slowly in the Christians who are called to influence this generation. We need to remember that the early church kept things very simple; they didn't run around looking for someone to help them get it right. Instead, they corrected each other according to the teachings of those who understood the Christian way the best at that time: the apostles—and even the apostles were not above correction.

When we are bearing the fruit of the Spirit to others, we exhibit Christ-like character; we are working on doing good works; we are faithful witnesses of our Lord; and we are givers just like our God, the greatest Giver who ever existed.

Stop Keep Transplanting Yourself

An olive tree is generally pretty resistant to being transplanted once it has established its root structure and begun to grow. This is interesting to think about because Christians are always transplanting themselves—moving from church to church, job to job, house to house, marriage to marriage, and friend to friend. When Jesus Christ sowed each one of us where we are, that is where we were needed at the time. God invests us into our areas of influence. He never invests anything of His into something with no value, which should give you an idea of how He values every living being.

> How He must long for us to bear fruit where we are sown, and to stop uprooting ourselves to look for ground that we think suits us better.

Christians move from church to church for so many soulish reasons: They have been offended; they feel that their talents are being overlooked; they feel ignored by the pastor, and on and on. Rooting down where I've been planted by God is simple for me because I have never embraced change joyfully. The few times I've moved since I became a Christian were definitely divine transplantings because I fussed and fidgeted all the way to my new destination.

God has had me planted in one church for most of the past thirty-three years, with the exception of two relatively short moves to other cities. I have seen many things—good and not so good. I've seen huge church complexes constructed outside of cities while the inner cities are dying one building at a time. The local church should not be a memorial to money and ambition. The local church should be a place of fellowship and refreshing, a training center that disciples believers so that they can go back outside of its walls to influence the generation in which they live. Instead, too many churches are like great barns providing safe storage for their seeds.

God's primary choice of communicating the Gospel has never been by satellite, by e-mail, or by tracts. He has always wanted to communicate His life, love, and hope to those in the world through us. The Word tells us this in John 3:16-17 (KJV):

> "God so loved the world, that he gave his only begotten Son, that whosoever believeth in him should not perish, but have everlasting life. For God sent not his Son into the world to condemn the world; but that the world through him might be saved."

Second Peter 3:9 (AMP) tells us this:

> "The Lord does not delay and is not tardy or slow about what He promises, according to some people's conception of slowness, but He is long-suffering (extraordinarily patient) toward you, not desiring

that any should perish, but that all should turn to repentance."

As He is waiting for the world to turn to repentance, it is time that we begin to mature in the growth process required that we might become fruitful fruit bearers.

Jesse Penn-Lewis makes a very interesting statement in her book, War on the Saints, stating that too many Christians are "surrendered in will, but not surrendered 'in fact,' in the sense of being ready to carry out obedience to the Holy Spirit at all costs." Being surrendered to God does not mean that you are now coated

> Being surrendered to God "in fact" means that you know when obstacles and hard things fall in your path, God can and will use them to enhance your purposes.

with Teflon and all problems and attacks will bead up and roll right off you. Being surrendered to God "in fact" as Jesse Penn Lewis says means that you are ready to move out and act upon whatever He sets before you. This will not always coincide with your plans or purposes, so your unsurrendered soul will probably try to find ways to avoid putting your surrender into action.

These Keys of the Kingdom do not mean that we now have keys to influence the world to run the way we think it

> Are you obeying God's Word regardless of the challenges Scripture makes to your comfort zone?

should. These Keys of the Kingdom mean that we have divine power to help us surrender to God's plans and purposes for our lives. Have you surrendered as fully as you are able to at this point in your life? Absolute obedience is the fruit of all genuine attempts to surrender. Is this fruit blossoming all over you and around you?

Are you worried that the consequences of your obedience might make you feel "out there" for others to take pot shots at? You and I will continue to have to make decisions and face challenges as long as we are on this earth. The great news is that the Keys of the Kingdom prayer principles make it possible to do this in direct accord with God's divine direction, divine empowerment, and divine blessing. Trouble, trials, and tribulations are not all going to magically disappear when you and I bind our wills to the will of God. Full surrender to God does not mean that you will never use your will again—the surrendered believer needs to continue choosing to act upon the choices he or she makes. With every prayer you pray and every confession of your faith that you make, there is usually a corresponding action you must take to imprint upon your soul the truth of your faith's commitment to that prayer.

In the learning experience of choosing to act upon your commitments to your prayers and your confessions of faith, you will often go through periods of time that will not always make sense to you. But you will find this waiting period easier and it seems to go by faster when you are binding your will to the will of God. How good it is to have the Word of God to explain such things to us. Romans 8:24-28 (TM) tells us this:

> *"That is why waiting does not diminish us, any more than waiting diminishes a pregnant mother. We are enlarged in the waiting. We, of course, don't see what is enlarging us. But the longer we wait, the larger we become, and the more joyful our expectancy. Meanwhile, the moment we get tired in the waiting, God's Spirit is right alongside helping us along. If we don't know how or what to pray, it doesn't matter. He*

does our praying in and for us, making prayer out of our wordless sighs, our aching groans. He knows us far better than we know ourselves, knows our pregnant condition, and keeps us present before God. That's why we can be so sure that every detail in our lives of love for God is worked into something good."

The really GREAT NEWS is that we can use the Keys of the Kingdom prayer principles to keep ourselves tied into God's will as it is established in heaven. Jesus wants us to now get ready to go into the recycling business with Him! He recycles the down and out, the broken, and the rebel. Let's get together with His schedule and forget ours. God's plans throughout time have certainly included you and me, but His plans are not all about us. Everyone in the body of Christ needs to regularly declare, "This is not about me, anymore. It's about them."

Summary

1. Human souls have been trying to blame anyone else but themselves for centuries.
2. When you are seeking the will of God to the best of your ability, His goodness, power, and love are always being worked in you, upon you, and through you out to the world.
3. The fruit of the Spirit as listed in the book of Galatians consists of "stuff" that is both something you *are* and something you *do*.
4. Always remember that the spiritual fruit you are bearing is the outward expression of how much Christ has been allowed to bear fruit in your soul.

5. Let us be faithful with the calling we have been given by Jesus Christ to go forth and bear fruit in this generation.

6. Too many people think if they starting acting better, then right thoughts will automatically appear in their minds. Too many changes that are being encouraged today are outward changes with no attempt to change the inward thoughts of the mind.

7. To take control over any part of our life, we must change our mind sets and our attitudes. It is easiest to do this when you first loose all wrong mind sets and wrong attitudes from your soul.

8. When we are bearing the fruit of the Spirit to others, this means we are exhibiting a Christ-like character, we are working on doing good works, we are a faithful witness of our Lord, and we are givers just like our God—the greatest Giver who ever existed.

9. When Jesus Christ sowed each one of us right where we are, that is where we were needed at the time. God invests us into our areas of influence.

10. These Keys of the Kingdom do not mean that we now have keys to influence the world to run the way we think it should. They mean that we have divine power to help us surrender to God's plans and purposes for our lives.

11. Absolute obedience is the fruit of all genuine attempts to surrender.

12. With every prayer you pray and every confession of your faith that you make, there is usually a corresponding action you must take to imprint upon your soul the truth of your faith's commitment to that prayer.

Chapter 10

Did You Ever See A Seed Walking?

Seeds Bear "Like Fruit," Not Strange Fruit

Parables compare abstract principles to tangible, known objects, changes, and processes so that people can understand what they are like. The Word of God says that as a believer you are good seed that has been ordained to bear much fruit. This is certainly an abstract statement. How are we like seeds and how are we going to bear fruit? Breaking down the process of a seed's destiny is a good place to start.

All fruit comes from a fruit-bearing tree or vine (plant, bush) that has come from the seed of like fruit. A tomato comes from a tomato plant, which came from a tomato seed, which came from a tomato. The seeds from a pinecone will produce pine trees, and the seeds from an ear of corn will produce corn. All fruit contains seed that will bear like fruit. When Christ was sown into the world, Christians were the fruit He produced.

God created men and women to reproduce themselves through a fruit-bearing process that is known as the fruit of the womb. God also created man and woman to produce fruit of another kind—fruit that is the result of, the product of, or the consequence of something a person has done. This kind of fruit has an influence that is much like the person who produced it. A kind, loving person will have a loving influence on others. An angry person will generally have an angry influence on others.

Jesus himself is the Incorruptible Seed who has rebirthed us as good seed. In 1 Peter 1:22-23 (NKJV), we read:

"Since you have purified your souls in obeying the truth through the Spirit in sincere love of the brethren, love one another fervently with a pure heart, having been born again, not of corruptible seed but incorruptible, through the word of God which lives and abides forever."

John 12:24 (NIV) tells us this:

"I tell you the truth, unless a kernel of wheat falls to the ground and dies, it remains only a single seed. But if it dies, it produces many seeds."

In Acts 3:25 (AMP) Peter said that through the Seed of Abraham, which is Christ, all the families and nations of the earth would be blessed:

"You are the descendants (sons) of the prophets and the heirs of the covenant which God made and gave to your forefathers, saying to Abraham, And in your Seed (Heir) shall all the families of the earth be blessed and benefited."

In John 15:16 (AMP) Jesus explained to His disciples that He had planted them in the world so they would produce fruit that would bless others:

"You have not chosen Me, but I have chosen you and I have appointed you [I have planted you], that you might go and bear fruit and keep on bearing, and that your fruit may be lasting [that it may remain, abide]."

And finally in Matthew 13:37-38 (NIV), Jesus explained the parable of the sower and the seed to His disciples:

"The one who sowed the good seed is the Son of Man. The field is the world, and the good seed stands for the sons of the kingdom."

Jesus is saying that the sons and daughters of the Kingdom, all Christians, would be sown into the world to bear fruit like Him. God sowed His Son, Jesus, into this world to influence humanity and produce fruit for His Kingdom. As Christians, Jesus has sown us into this world to influence humanity in the age in which we live and to produce fruit for His Kingdom. We are planted right where we are to bear good fruit through the consequences of our actions and our influence.

What Happens When Good Seed Has Been Sown?

Certain seeds are fruit bearers in embryo form, filled with an energy that is only released when their environment is correct. Seeds have germination inhibitors in them, which prevent them from germinating until their chances of survival are good. To germinate means to start coming into existence; to become something great out of something

> God placed inhibitors in seeds to make sure that they would not try to sprout until they were sown into the soil where they had the best chance of bearing fruit.

very small. Without these inhibitors, a tomato seed would sprout right inside the tomato containing it. As long as these germination inhibitors are active, the seed remains dormant.

Spring-like conditions in the soil into which a seed is sown—water and warmth, longer days and stronger sunlight—signal the seed to break its dormancy. Water does two things to a seed. First, it activates enzymes that stimulate the release of food energy stored in the seed. Second, it splits the tough seed coat open so that oxygen gets inside the seed. Energy stored in the seed to power its cells to divide and grow can only burn in the presence of oxygen. This process is called *respiration*, which also means to breathe in and out.

The germinating seed's stored energy only lasts so long. That's why a sprouting seed has to unfold into the light as quickly as it can. If a small seed germinates in a moist but dark environment, it can run out of energy before it ever finds its way to the light.

Before a seed begins to grow up into its destiny, it must first anchor itself with its root system. Roots serve a double function: They anchor the new growth coming up out of the seed, and they absorb water and food to nourish the new shoot that grows from the seed. As the shoot begins to grow, it splits the seed coat even more and pushes its way up above the soil. As the root continues to grow, the first leaves will grow on the new shoot, which enable the plant to begin to produce energy using the sun's light.

And last, but not least, when you look at the inside or end of most seeds, you will observe a small scar similar to a belly button. This is where the seed was attached to the fruit that contained it. Isn't it wonderful how God has explained His plans and purposes for us through Jesus Christ's parables using agricultural processes which every tongue and tribe of the earth of all times could understand?

Seeing Ourselves in the Fruit Bearing Process

New Christians are potential fruit bearers in embryo form, filled with a divine energy that is released when they are finally in God's chosen environment of influence. The new life rising up within each believer after his or her new birth can be likened to seeds showing signs of life in the spring. In the spring, water is readily available and longer days and stronger sunlight cause seeds to begin to sprout.

If we liken water to the Word of God, we can see how His Word stimulates the release of the divine energy stored within our souls. The Word also splits open the hard shells of our souls that have enabled us to hide from our true purposes. That shell has to break open so God's breath of life gets inside us and begins to grow us into branches that will bear fruit. Divine energy in us will only start burning in His presence.

Each potential fruit bearer walks a different path that is unique from other seeds' paths. God has

> Without these divine inhibitors, we might begin trying to produce fruit before our foundation roots were ready to withstand the attacks of the enemy.

also set a different time frame in each of our purposes. Just as seeds have little things in them called germination inhibitors, which prevent them from sprouting until their chances of survival are good, so He has placed divine inhibitors in us until we are ready to burst forth with fruit. This may be why some believers feel stifled and fruitless at times—they haven't yet accepted their soil or put down strong roots in their area of influence.

Most seeds have a small scar similar to a belly button (especially in a bean or a peanut). This is where the seed was attached to the fruit that birthed it. What a marvelous analogy that seems to be—each one of us having a spiritual belly button where we were first attached to the divine Good Seed.

The Seasons of Fruit Bearing

Spring, summer, fall, and winter—each season has a different flavor, a different smell, and a different purpose. Ecclesiastes 3:1-8 (TM) tells us that:

> *"There's an opportune time to do things, a right time*
> *for everything on the earth:*
> *A right time for birth and another for death,*
> *A right time to plant and another to reap,*
> *A right time to kill and another to heal,*
> *A right time to destroy and another to construct,*
> *A right time to cry and another to laugh,*
> *A right time to lament and another to cheer,*
> *A right time to make love and another to abstain,*
> *A right time to embrace and another to part,*
> *A right time to search and another to count your losses,*
> *A right time to hold on and another to let go,*
> *A right time to rip out and another to mend,*
> *A right time to shut up and another to speak up,*
> *A right time to love and another to hate,*
> *A right time to wage war and another to make peace."*

While the above verses are sure to have divine, prophetic meanings, they have ordinary daily life meanings as well. If we do not learn to flow with these times of change in our lives, we will drive ourselves crazy while we try to change them. We cannot change the times and the seasons around us, but we can cooperate with them.

I once heard someone say, "Plan your life as if you were going to live to be one hundred years old—but live every single day as if it were your last." We must always remember that God is control of every coming and passing of our lives. We can only control how we view and react to the changes that come our way.

If we looked at the seasons of our fruit bearing as we would at the natural seasons, it would be simple to say that many of us are past springtime and should have fully established branches

> There you stand, pruned and filled with purpose.

by now. Perhaps you've been working through the blistering heat of summer to get rid of your unnecessary parts and branches, a kind of self-pruning through the binding and loosing prayers. Life's seasons don't always seem to follow the order of the natural seasons, so perhaps you have also experienced some dark wintry times of feeling cold and far from bearing any fruit during your other seasons. Your fall season of harvest may not have even come into view.

We all need to begin to look at our season of fruit bearing as being all the time—365, 24, and 7. You will go through natural and spiritual seasons, but you will be capable of bearing fruit in the heat of the summer and in the cold snows of the winter. Olive trees have been around for nearly forever. These trees need full sun for fruit production, but they also need a slight winter chill for their fruit to set. That is an interesting analogy for the Christian who bears fruit that is the sweetest when he or she has walked through hard, cold times and come out the other side in victory.

Olive trees tend to grow dense, thin branches that need to be pruned heavily to bear the most fruit. The fruit of the olives can be handpicked, gathered with a special wooden rake-like tool, or harvested by hitting the branches with long poles. This is an interesting similarity to Christians. Too often, we don't want to give out our fruit, and we must be whacked with God's long poles to release a harvest of any kind.

Remember what hard times work out in us as Paul says in Romans 5:3-5 (TM):

> *"There's more to come: We continue to shout our praise even when we're hemmed in with troubles, because we know how troubles can develop passionate patience in us, and how that patience in turn forges the tempered steel of virtue, keeping us alert for whatever God will do next. In alert expectancy such as this, we're never left feeling shortchanged. Quite the contrary—we can't round up enough containers to hold everything God generously pours into our lives through the Holy Spirit!"*

Troubles and tribulations develop passionate patience in us. What a paradoxical phrase, "passionate patience." Patience is a capacity to tolerate delay, trouble, or suffering without becoming angry or upset; to be able to persevere calmly when faced with difficulties; to be able to tolerate being hurt, provoked, or annoyed without complaining or losing one's temper. Patience is not just the knack of waiting; it requires tolerance, perseverance, calmness, no complaining, and a steady temperament. Yet, to be passionate means to have very intense feelings about something.

A good disposition is vital to fruit bearing because the potential fruit can be rather testy and touchy at times.

Are these words at complete odds with each other? No, because a passionate person who feels very strongly about things can learn to face difficulties with tolerance, perseverance, and a good disposition. This is the model for Christians who are in their winter season—they can be practicing their godly attributes and perfecting their dispositions. The passionate person is tempered and trained through delay to move with God in His perfect timing. Developing a capacity for patience helps to smooth off the rough edges of some of the more passionate Christians' tendency to be quick tempered, uncontrollably exuberant, and energetic to the point of getting on peoples' nerves.

Your influence on the people in the world around you involves many opportunities. In fact, there are hundreds of opportunities every day where you can begin to bear fruit. Think of the world as just one big orchard. The first thing you need to do is get rid of your "us versus them" attitude. There is no "us versus them" in God's eyes. He loves all mankind. As His fruit bearers, we are expected to be impacting Christians, non-Christians, alcoholics, airline pilots, Jehovah's Witnesses, veterinarians, park rangers, Mormons, hair dressers, Muslims, teachers, New Age adherents, rap singers, plumbers, homosexuals and lesbians, teenagers, prostitutes, cab drivers, writers, drug addicts, difficult neighbors, and senior citizens. While this is not a complete list by any means, it should give you a working idea of your world, your generation, and your area of influence.

Guard Your Mornings

Guard your mornings. Carve out time in the earliest part of each day to spend with the Lord. We tend to fill up our minds (already cluttered with misconceptions of every size and color) with schedules, social activities, concerns we worry about, work, our families, the media bombardment of terrorism, rumors of war,

> It is easy to get caught up in the frenzy of these factors and neglect spiritual things when you have a partially unsurrendered mind.

economic collapse, and violence. These are the factors that our spirit, soul, and body come in contact with every day. There are thousands and thousands of Christians in this state, and not one of them lives in overcoming victory!

Someone once complained to me that nobody seemed to want to pray anymore. There just wasn't enough prayer in the church, yada yada yada. When she finished, I said, "We have a prayer meeting every Tuesday. Would you like to come to it?" I knew what I would hear back because Christians often complain about the problems in the Church without really wanting to spend the time and energy to be a part of the solutions. They just remain a complaining part of the problem.

The woman quickly replied, "Oh, you do? I'll bet it's a great prayer meeting. I really don't know, though, I'm awfully busy right now. I'll see if I can fit it into my schedule."

I replied, "If you are going to try to make the prayer meeting fit into your schedule, it will never happen. You'll never find time. You need to prioritize what is important in life and schedule the prayer meeting first, that is if it's important. If you are really concerned that no one seems to be praying for this area, commit to the two hours of this prayer meeting each week and make the rest of your life fall in around that time. You will still have 166 hours left over each week."

> You have to take the first fruits of your week by force and give them to fruit bearing.

The enemy will never let you find spare hours during your week where you can go and influence others for the Kingdom of God. If you decide to give time each week—two, three, or five hours or whatever—begin to think about how you will spend it. At first, you may need to dig out your own ways to spend those few hours—but that won't last long. Trust me, the world is starving for some attention, someone to listen, and for just some plain old TLC.

The Church and the Seeds

In Matthew's Gospel, we read that Jesus explained the following to His disciples about the parable of the seed and the sower (Matthew 13:37-38, NIV):

> *"The one who sowed the good seed is the Son of Man. The field is the world, and the good seed stands for the sons of the kingdom."*

Jesus said He was going to sow the sons and daughters of the Kingdom into the world to bear fruit. He has cast you and me into the world to bear fruit wherever He has chosen to plant us. God sowed His Son into this world to influence all humanity and to produce fruit for the Kingdom. We have been sown into this world at this time to influence humanity in the age in which we live and to produce fruit for the Kingdom.

God has determined that we should finish the works that Jesus left for us to do after He went back to be with His Father in heaven. You and I have been sown into the world where God wants us, and I don't know about you—but I want to grow and bloom and then sprout fruit like crazy right there.

We go to church to learn of the Word, to be discipled, to have godly fellowship, and to be trained for greater purposes. Unfortunately, some of us have been taught to avoid mingling

> Our main sphere of influence should be out in the world.

with those in the world—yet the world is our mission field! Notice in Matthew 13:38 where the owner's servants asked the owner if they should pull up the tares (weeds) that an enemy had sown into his field overnight. The owner said to leave them alone and let the harvesters deal with them at the time of the harvest.

The field of this owner represents the world, and the tares represent unbelievers. We are not to judge the tares and put them away from us. The harvesters (angels) at the end of the age will deal with those who are still unbelievers when Christ returns. Until He does, we are to influence potential wheat and tares alike while always hoping that some of the tares might come over to God's side.

Never forget that it is the world where you are called to influence others and bear fruit. Don't be one of those who will never bear fruit sitting in the pews of their churches—your soil is the world. You will never bear fruit in your easy chair in a darkened room in front of a television set or a computer screen. You will only bear mushrooms there. The Bible never said, "Go forth and bear fungi!" Bear fruit out in the world, my brothers and sisters, bear fruit out in the world.

How Do You Start Bearing Fruit?

You must first fully surrender yourself to the fruit-bearing process. You have already been sown into the soil of the world. But you may have managed to get into a place where the light is not shining brightly enough and the water of the Word has not yet soaked into you. You are not germinating. Pray this prayer to move back into the light's shining and the water's soaking.

Your Word says I am good seed, Lord. Good seed ultimately produces good fruit that lasts forever. I don't want to be unfruitful; I want to bear bushels of fruit for the Kingdom. I choose to totally obligate my will to your will and your purposes, Father. I choose to totally obligate my mind to your mind's thought processes, Jesus. I bind all of my emotions to your healing balance, Holy Spirit, because I need them truly balanced and prepared to be able to love and influence the most difficult fruit. I loose every single one of my self-rights, self-agendas, and self-motives. Show me what else I need to loose to cause my soul to surrender completely to you. Show me whatever may be in the way of my being one with your purposes, Lord. I will give them all up. I know I'm close to walking in my destiny purposes. Show me how to take the first step, how to influence my generation and age. I commit everything I am and all I have to you. Amen.

When you surrender yourself to becoming a fruit bearer, you will be fulfilled as never before, and the fruit will be eternally grateful. In John 15:16 (AMP), Jesus tells each one of us:

> "You have not chosen Me, but I have chosen you and I have appointed you [I have planted you], that you might go and bear fruit and keep on bearing, and that your fruit may be lasting [that it may remain, abide], so that whatever you ask the Father in My Name [as presenting all that I AM], He may give it to you."

Have a Vision for Fruit

It is not difficult to reach those who are broken and crying for help. They have given up because they have no hope that things will ever get any better. The harder cases are the ones who are apathetic, in denial, self-sufficient, or full of rebellion. This describes some church congregations as well as unbelievers.

Unbelievers reject offers of help because they are too proud, they've been rejected before, they don't believe God exists, they aren't sure Christianity will work for them, their parents made them go to church too much when they were little, and so on. They have had all understanding blocked from their blinded minds. Second Corinthians 4:4 (TM) describes their situation:

> *"All they have eyes for is the fashionable god of darkness. They think he can give them what they want, and that they won't have to bother believing a Truth they can't see. They're stone-blind to the dayspring brightness of the Message that shines with Christ, who gives us the best picture of God we'll ever get."*

You need to get a personal vision for bearing fruit. Having a vision lets you see beyond what your natural sight would see. Vision sees the answers; natural sight only sees the problems. Once as I drove to a meeting in the extreme northern part of California, and suddenly I rounded a bend and crested a hill and the gorgeous, snow-covered Mount Shasta (a dormant volcano) came into view—all 14,162 feet of it!

When I returned the next day, a rather unusual optical illusion intrigued me.

A few miles northwest of Mount Shasta is a neighboring dormant volcano vent called Black Butte because it looks very black and ominous to the natural eye. It stands just over 6,000 feet tall. I did not see the less famous Black Butte until I had driven completely past Mount Shasta—the smaller mountain being hidden behind the bigger one. As I was driving back from the meeting and heading towards Black Butte, I saw that it was going to completely obscure the much bigger Mount Shasta until I finally got past it. About fifteen minutes later, Mount

Shasta suddenly loomed into view. The smaller mountain had completely covered my view of the magnificent Mount Shasta until I managed to go around it.

How often do we look at a large dark problem and that is all we see? We stop moving and don't even try to get past it. We only see the darkness of the problem. Black Butte prevented me from seeing the glorious, snow-covered Mt. Shasta, but I had a vision in my mind of what Mt. Shasta looked like. I wanted to see it, and as I kept moving towards it on the freeway, suddenly there it was. When we have a vision of the answer, we don't get discouraged by the black mountain of problem that we see with our natural eyes. Vision is about seeing what God wants us to see instead of what the world sees.

Your vision will help you get past the things that your soul might think of to prevent you from influencing your part of the world. Keep a picture in your heart of being covered with big thick clusters of grapes. Or peaches, or bananas—whatever makes you think of being a fruit bearer. Then start with just one small step. Here's a suggested list of things you can do as an individual to begin to bear fruit.

- Pray and ask God to direct you
- Make phone calls for senior organizations
- Make phone calls to latch key kids
- Find a need in your area and fill it
- Find your area's hurt and do something to help it heal
- Think about what you need that would make your life better if someone would do it for you

There is a gift in each one of us that is to be manifested for the good. Don't look for programs to implement, look for the outlet for an expression of your gift. Look for the needs, or talk to people in your area and ask them what their needs are.

- Get out in your community and walk around—don't have preconceived notions about what people need while thinking you are the answer
- Don't forget they already have a Savior waiting to meet them; you're just His messenger
- Learn to be a good listener wherever you are
- Visit neighbors who live alone
- Go out in the neighborhood and offer donuts and coffee on Saturday morning and ask the neighbors how they are doing
- Offer to pray with distressed people in the park or at a mall
- Go out every week to a certain block from 10 to 12 in the morning, knock on their doors and tell them you were just in the neighborhood picking up trash, and then ask them if there is anything you could do for them
- Create an expectation that you'll be back and then GO BACK

> I was very intrigued by the New Testament Church model that this entire congregation was living.

What can a church do to impact a distressed neighborhood? I am blessed with two friends in Cherry Hill, New Jersey: Pastors Kyle and Danielle Horner of River of Life Worship Center. I spoke at their church in November of 2004 and instantly felt a bonding to these two dynamic pioneers. This church has an outreach program to a distressed part of a nearby city that is mind-boggling. Just prior to finalizing this chapter, I interviewed both of them and their associate Pastor James (who heads up River of Life Worship Center's new Dream Center in this city).

The outreach leaders carefully researched the history of this city, trying to find out why a certain section was so distressed and what had caused it to be that way. They learned that people who could afford to all started moving to the suburbs after World War II. The poorest people were left behind. Wherever there is a concentration of great poverty, violence flourishes. Where violence flourishes, hope hides and gives up.

My first question to them was, "How did you start this outreach?" They went out to find where the people of this area had an itch. "No use scratching where there's no itch," Pastor Kyle said. To find the itch, they began walking around the area and meeting the people long before they were ready to start the thrust of the outreach. They knocked on doors and asked what they could do for people. They picked up trash on the street and handed out donuts and coffee to the drug dealers on the corners. They said nothing about anybody getting saved; they weren't packing witnessing tracts; they didn't carry any Bibles.

River of Life Worship Center is based upon the premise that trust comes out of relationship—without relationship, unity of vision and purpose is hard to achieve. People won't care how much you know until they know you care. Once the people of the neighborhood learned to trust Pastors Kyle and James (a former drug user eight years earlier), the people began to tell these men what they needed—help with dealing with a school, disposable diapers for a new baby, a job, etc.

The drug people in the area began to respect these men because they realized they were not in conflict with them, but instead were trying to pick up the neighborhood and help their own families.

Pastor Kyle says there are a lot of problems in distressed neighborhoods, and the people are living the way they are because they have no hope. You can speak of Jesus' love and the hope He gives, but if the people you are talking to don't have any food to eat or any shoes to wear, love and hope are abstract concepts to them. Pastors Kyle and James found out that there were a lot of reasons the people were living in poverty and pushing drugs. One dealer had found a good job, but was fired when the business owners found out he had a prison record. He said he had to feed his family, and drug pushing was the only thing he could do to guarantee that his family would eat.

So, these two pastors began to visit business people to tell them that they would get the people in church and teach them to be trustworthy—then they could trust them enough to hire them. Pastor Kyle urged the businesses in the area to try to employ the people they wouldn't normally hire. He reminded people that Jesus preached every day, but it wasn't until after He fed the people that they flocked around Him and wanted to make Him King. When He raised Lazarus from the dead, people were finally ready to believe in Him because they saw a tangible expression of His love and power.

Pastor Kyle and Danielle stress that exampling of the truth and preaching of the Word are both necessary. The truth is powerful, but a tangible example of the truth brings transformation. Telling people that they have value and their Father in heaven wants them to know they are loved is good. Showing them that you value them and God loves them by painting their houses and repairing their windows makes a connection with them. The people won't care much about abstract explanations and teaching until they see the principle in action. Then you will have their attention.

The church has put the cart before the horse, these pastors say. When a church sends out witnessing teams, they keep offering answers to questions that nobody is asking. The key to generating the questions first is to show them that someone cares about them with no hidden motives. Pastor Kyle says that it is effective to just walk around neighborhoods and meet the people. No preaching, no tracts, no tiny New Testaments. Just a cup of coffee and a concerned question about their lives. After a few Saturdays of this, people will start asking the questions and then it time to begin giving the answers.

Both Pastor Kyle and Danielle have stressed to their people right from the beginning that working with their Adopt-a-Block

> They taught their people about not fearing those who were different from them, that God had created them all the same way.

program required commitment—in fact, they asked for a year's commitment from everyone who joined the team. They taught their team that the people of value they were going to minister to just needed to see love and hope in action—they needed visible caring for them to care about what the team was doing.

The night that River of Life Worship Center was going to kick off its new city church at the Dream Center, there was a crisis in the city. Crisis does not have to be your enemy; it can be a divine opportunity to express love, and influence the people in the crisis says Pastor Kyle.

A large truck hit and broke a major sewer line and raw sewage began spilling into the area's drinking water supply. The Adopt-a-Block team was supposed to start their city church the very night the water crisis burst onto the scene, but instead they did a radical thing. They postponed their opening night and the ministry team went out and got bottles of water to take to the people in the neighborhood. That night the team decided to *be the church* instead of trying to open the church.

The pastors spoke of a teenage girl (eighteen years old) named Boots who had been studying sign language—but she felt she had no gifts to offer anyone. When she went to help with the Adopt-a-Block ministry team for the first time, the first door she knocked on was opened by a deaf man. She had been afraid that she couldn't sign well enough to help anybody, and God put her right in the face of a man who needed to know what these people were doing in the neighborhood.

The pastors asked her to start a signing service at the church, but she was still afraid that she didn't know how to sign well enough to do that. Pastor Kyle told her that the deaf people who now wanted to come to their church would get more out of the service if she signed what she knew than they would without anyone trying to share their gift.

Recently, as the team was walking around the block inviting people to come visit the new city church, a drug addict wanted to know who they were. He wanted to know if they were a cult. They said no, they were from the Dream Center in the area. He immediately recognized that name and said, "You're the people who fixed up that house on Donovan Street in 24 hours, aren't you?" They immediately had his trust because he knew about their tangible expression of love to the people in the run down house on Donovan Street.

Their ministry team did a 24-Hour Miracle Makeover (their name) on this house, fixing broken boards, painting the house, putting on new doors, patching the roof, and many other expression of caring. They modeled a tangible way to express love to the people of the area, so they could then tell them that Christ does miracle makeovers on broken, hopeless people, too.

Pastor Danielle felt that it was very important that the people understand the heart behind the vision. These pastors spent both time and effort to give the people of the area time to trust them, always showing them complete respect for their worth and their value. Pastor Kyle said they knew they had to go into the vision believing the people were incredibly valuable to God. Both Pastors Kyle and Danielle said it was urgent to always speak the language of just "us," never them and us, never Cherry Hill and their city, just us—over and over. They preached about breaking down the wall of fear, breaking down ignorance about each other.

> They preached a year and a half about loving all people because they were Jesus' people.

Pastors Kyle and Danielle offer this list of points to remember whenever undertaking reaching out to any neighborhood:

- The Kingdom of God is not about you; it is about others. If you see yourself as an important volunteer who is doing a good charitable thing, you will fail.
- Compassion is not a philosophy, not a subject to teach; it is an action. Without compassion, everything else is a program.
- You must see the value of those around you—there is great value to God beneath the addictions, the dirt, and the alcohol.
- No church is the church it needs to be until its people see other people as those who just need to get on track with God.
- God is a wise investor. He doesn't invest us into people unless He sees their potential.
- Keep looking up at the Hand that is sowing you into the world.

- You are not the sower; you are the seed. Just be a good seed and grow until you bear fruit.
- Bind yourself to God's concept of the situation around your church or your neighborhood and loose preconceived ideas you have about those areas.
- Our self-image and sense of worth are warped by our own self-layers of protection and need that we have from all the traumatic things we have gone through. We need a good God image.
- We are the moon; He is the Sun. We have no light of our own; we just reflect His light.

For those of you who would like a better understanding of reaching out to your own neighborhoods, Pastors Kyle and Danielle Horner have graciously agreed to provide whatever information they can to help you get started.

River of Life Dream Center
856-488-6322
www.ROLWC.org (click on Dream Center)

NOW, Start Focusing on Just Doing It!

Here we are at the end, but hopefully this is your beginning of new thoughts and feelings about bearing fruit in your generation. You are a good seed ready to be walking, talking, and loving others. It is time for you to begin to bear fruit, both within your own character and in the lives of those you were born to influence.

He has given you all that you need: the Keys of the Kingdom prayer principles, your game plan as a good seed, and His promises and power to back you up. Go and bear fruit for your Father above. Know that all of your answers can be found in His Word, and that He hears every word of prayer that you breathe out. God is for you.

The only thing left to do now is for me to pray for you as you have finished this book and hopefully begun to think about germinating and sprouting and growing up towards the Son.

> Lord, I thank you for this awesome opportunity to encourage your good seed. I bind each person who reads these words to your will, to the mind of Christ, and to the healing balance of the Holy Spirit. I bind their feet to the paths that you ordained for them to walk since the foundation of the earth. I bind their hands to the work that you have ordained them to do. Give them strength and encouragement to go and be and do. Pour grace and mercy out upon them, and show them what to do to bear all of the luscious fruit of your Spirit. I loose, smash, crush, and destroy all the works of the enemy from them and their spheres of influence. I loose all doubt and fear from them that might try to keep them from producing great bushels of fruit. Bless your seed, Jesus, bless your seed. Thank you for sowing us all into the world! Thank you for wanting us to work with you in the preparation of the greatest harvest ever. Thank you for everything! Amen.

Summary

1. God sowed His Son into this world to influence humanity and produce fruit for His Kingdom. As Christians, Jesus has sown us into this world to influence humanity in the age in which we live and produce fruit for His Kingdom.

2. We are planted right where we are to bear good fruit through the consequences of our actions and our influence.

3. Each potential fruit bearer walks a different path that is unique from other paths. God has also set an individual time frame for each of our purposes.

4. We cannot change the times and the seasons around us, but we can cooperate with them.

5. We all need to begin to look at our season of fruit bearing as being all the time—365, 24, and 7.

6. Troubles and tribulations should always develop passionate patience in us.

7. The passionate person is tempered and trained through delay to move with God in His perfect timing.

8. Guard your mornings. Carve out time in the earliest part of each day to spend it with the Lord.

9. God has determined that we would finish the works that Jesus left for us to do after He went back to be with His Father in heaven.

10. You need to get a personal vision for bearing fruit.

11. Vision is about seeing what God wants us to see instead of what the world sees.

12. You are a good seed walking, talking, and loving others. It is time for you to begin to bear fruit within your own character and in the lives of those you were born to influence.

Other Books by Liberty Savard

Shattering Your Strongholds

Shattering Your Strongholds Workbook

Breaking the Power

Breaking the Power Workbook

Producing the Promise

*Keys to Understanding:
Freedom Here and Now*

*Keys to Understanding:
Relationships*

*Keys to Understanding:
Soul Ties, Soul Power, and Soulish Prayers*

*Keys to Understanding:
Spiritual Understanding and Warfare*

Fear Not America

Apples of Gold in Baskets of Silver

The Unsurrendered Soul

Contact Liberty for speaking engagements, seminars,
and schools at:

Liberty Savard Ministries
P.O. Box 41260
Sacramento CA 95841
916-721-7770
www.libertysavard.com